LESSONS AT BLACKBERRY INN

Adventures with the Gentle Art of Learning™

Karen Andreola

ILLUSTRATED BY
NIGEL ANDREOLA

Charlotte Mason
Research & Supply
Company

Lessons at Blackberry Inn: Adventures with the Gentle Art of Learning™
Copyright ©2009 Karen Andreola
All rights reserved

Illustrations by Nigel Andreola
Cover cross stitch by Karen Andreola
Cover Design by Pine Hill Graphics
Interior Design by Pine Hill Graphics

Publisher's Cataloging-in-Publication Data
(Provided by Cassidy Cataloguing Services, Inc.)

Andreola, Karen.

 Lessons at Blackberry Inn : adventures with the gentle art of
 learning / Karen Andreola ; illustrated by Nigel Andreola. --
 Quarryville, Pa. : Charlotte Mason Research & Supply Co., c2009.

  p. ; cm.
  ISBN: 978-1-889209-05-0

  1. Homemakers--United States--1901-1953--Fiction. 2. Home
 schooling--United States--Fiction. 3. Hotelkeepers--United States--
 Fiction. 4. Conduct of life--Fiction. I. Andreola, Nigel. II. Title.

PS3601.N5497 L47 2009
813/.6--dc22   0904

Printed in the United States of America.

Contents

Preface

$\mathcal{I}$ believe an author of children's fiction has a duty to describe the world as it ought to be, as it can be.

You might be thinking, "But this is a book for grown-ups, isn't it?"

Yes, it is. And in it I aim to demonstrate that the "idyllic principle" is also applicable to stories for grown-ups. For all fiction is useful chiefly to animate truth, to inspire some noble aim or sweet spirit. Therefore, it is for your enrichment that I have created scenes of faith, hope, patience, industry, trust, generosity, hospitality, parental love, and the love between a married man and woman—all of which are meant to quicken your heart. But please don't take the story too seriously. If you find anything silly, feel free to laugh. Laughter is medicine with good side effects.

Gone are the days when close friends lived within walking distance. Do you ever read as a remedy for feeling a bit lonely? I do. If we read fiction for its characters, then I invite you to make friends of my characters because I created them especially for mothers like you. In this story life is seen through Carol's eyes, the eyes of a homemaker in the 1930s. Those things that pertain to mother and home abound here. In fact, the forgotten value of homemaking fills every nook and cranny. May these pages inspire you to take part in what I call Mother Culture™, to nourish your soul, and to imbue your home with an atmosphere of love, beauty, purity, and good works.

This story also ministers with specific ideas for teaching children. Behind Carol's decisions is a teaching philosophy and a method that I call "The Gentle Art of Learning™." It is my interpretation of what can be found in *Home Education*, a book written in the nineteenth century by the British Christian, Miss Charlotte Mason. I first read *Home Education* in 1986 while living in England, borrowing an old copy through London's interlibrary loan program. Still in the beginning stages of teaching my young children, and with only a handful of books to help me, I was hungrily searching for ideas. In *Home Education* I found the specifics I was craving, and so does my main character, Carol. She finds the philosophy inspiring and tailors the method to fit her situation, her children, and her particular tastes, thus supplying you with an inside look at how one mother makes personal The Gentle Art of Learning.

Karen Andreola
Autumn 2008

Chapter One

My Liberty

*Bread and
butter, devoid
of charm in the
drawing room, is
ambrosia eaten
under a tree.*
Elizabeth von Antrim

The church bell had rung hours ago but I was still in bed. I was reading, taking in my last days of recuperation—doctor's orders. Expecting a child and being prone to miscarry, I had been confined to bed rest after a fall down the attic steps two weeks prior. By this time I had memorized every crack in the walls and the way the sun cast polka-dot shadows through the eyelet curtains every day at two o'clock. Outside my windows a pair of cardinals kept me daily company. They were hidden in the trees, but I recognized their distinct tweets, and though they were lacking in melody, I was comforted by their sweet and simple conversation.

I heard someone climbing the long staircase. It could have been one of the weekend guests here at Blackberry Inn, but it wasn't. It was Emma.

At her knock, I called, "Come in."

"You're looking well, Carol," she said. She placed a glass of lemonade and an envelope on my nightstand and then gently patted my shoulder.

"I'm feeling well, thank you," I said, returning her smile. I watched her sweep a few stray light brown and gray hairs away from her damp forehead and gracefully fasten them back in place.

"Did you walk home from church?" I asked.

"Yes, it's a beautiful Sunday for a walk and only just getting warm." Her mention of the outdoors drew her soft hazel eyes to the windows, where she immediately began fussing with the curtains, drawing them further open to make visible the wonders that lay beyond. The maples glowed bright green in the midday sun. "Michael

was still talking with the men when I set off, probably planning what the quartet will sing next," she added.

"Was it a good sermon?" I asked.

"Yes. Pastor Bingham preached on diligence, mostly out of the Psalms. He also quoted something from John Wesley. Let's see, what was it? Oh, yes. 'Though I am always in haste, I am never in a hurry.' I like that, don't you?"

"I've never heard that one," I said.

"Nor have I," she said. "Oh, and he threw in some Ben Franklin for good measure, for the children, I think. 'One today is worth two tomorrows; never leave till tomorrow what you can do today,' and the like."

"Hmm," I sighed, and lay quiet. Emma did one last bit of fussing. Bending over to the floor, she tidied the pile of books by my bed, stacking them in order—the largest at the bottom, the smallest at the top, forming a pyramid. As she straightened up, she asked, "Can I get you anything else, dear?"

The subject of the sermon still lingered in my thoughts. "No, thank you," I answered demurely. I felt a tinge of frustration. Emma and I always served the Sunday meal together. Now Emma was doing extra work while I remained in bed, yet her servant's heart voiced no hint of complaint.

"Now, Carol, I know what you're thinking."

"You do?" I asked, but she ignored this.

"You have *not* been idle. You've been keeping the baby safe. And you've been diligent even in bed. Just look at all these books you've been reading in preparation for teaching the children. You know how to use your time wisely." She carefully lifted my knitting out of its basket. "And look at this pretty sweater. What a lovely rose color!" I had been knitting a cardigan for my daughter, Emily, and was particular about my pinks. Emma held it up to admire it in the sunbeams that streamed in through the windows. It did look pretty in the sunlight, or was it Emma's encouragement that made me appreciate it more? I felt gratified. "You're nearly done," she said, returning it to its nesting place, leaving it with another of her affectionate pats.

"Oh yes," she continued, "I almost forgot. Dora sends her greetings. The note on the nightstand is from her. Michael and the children should be here any minute." The announcement to me seemed to reinforce her contentment with her decision to have us move in with her. Her words trailed behind her as she set off to do the proverbial "next thing."

I sipped my lemonade. The water comes up so cold from our deep well that no ice is needed to chill it. With a squeeze of lemon, a teaspoon of sugar, and a sprig of peppermint, it is welcome refreshment on warm days. As I sipped, I thanked God for His blessings, demonstrated to me through Mrs. Emma Cook, proprietor of Blackberry Inn, best friend to my mother in days gone by, my childhood Sunday school teacher—as well as everyone else's, and the adopted grandmother to my little boy and girl. Emma's generosity had been established by habit. I knew she often visited the widows and sick of our congregation. She had the rock-hard calves of a frequent walker and cyclist to prove it.

I gingerly opened the envelope, addressed to "Mrs. Michael Weaver" in neat Spenserian handwriting. Inside was a pretty invitation framed in orange marigolds, water-colored by Dora's hand, flowers apropos of the season. We rarely receive formal invitations out here in the country. Although Dora has willingly taken on country life by marrying my brother Bob and lives with him on Dad's old dairy farm, she was city-bred, and formal invitations were evidently in the blood. I was looking forward immensely to tea with Dora, and found intriguing the sentence about teaching my little Emily and me something new.

Michael and I were hired by Emma this July to be caretakers and assistant innkeepers of Blackberry Inn—a large white clapboard house nestled in the first ripples of wooded hills that touch the Appalachian

Mountains of New England. Although built on the edge of two hundred acres, Blackberry Inn is nevertheless a comfortable walking distance from the center of the village of Appleton. Appleton hasn't changed much. Here I was raised and here I had returned with my own family. Moving back here wasn't my idea; I suspected a conspiratorial effort on the part of my brother Bob, my husband Michael, and Emma. In fact, I found out only recently that for quite some time Michael has secretly harbored romantic notions of country living. In reality I know it is a life governed by the four seasons and requiring a strong back.

Twenty-five miles easterly, as the crow flies, is Bridgeton, a larger town that the people of Appleton call "the city," where Michael once held a position in the marketing department of a growing company. Bridgeton is where we met and started a family before disappointing circumstances led us here. But we've put the burdens that darkened

those days behind us. Our children, Donald and Emily, like our life in Appleton. They have made the otherwise neglected apple orchard behind the inn their expansive playground. Although I appreciated our life in Bridgeton, watching the children's energetic games, the calling, running, and climbing of country play, was helping me to accept our new life here.

I got up. I couldn't bear to be in bed any longer. Monday was to be my first day on my feet but after all I was only stealing a few hours of early liberty, I rationalized. I brushed my hair, fastening a hair comb on either side. That was all that could be done on short notice. After changing into something less wrinkled, I peeked in at the children's room. What a mess! "I'll tackle that later," I thought, "with their help."

Halfway down the stairs I met Michael. He looked handsome in his finely tailored brown suit, which blended with the darker brown of his hair.

"Carol, you're up!" he exclaimed, surprised.

"Yes, I know tomorrow is supposed to be my day up but..." His dark eyes conveyed "never mind," and he reached for my hand with the decorum of a gentleman leading me onto a dance floor, placing it in the crook of his elbow.

"Of course. Today is a beautiful day," he finished for me. We walked arm in arm toward the kitchen.

The children came bounding in. "Hi, Mommy!" they both called out. I gave them each a hug. "Hands washed?" I asked. Without a word they headed for the sink. I was happy to see that Donald let his younger sister go first, and I was content that not another reminder of manners was needed by me on that point.

Emma's dining room table was long and the meals longer, when guests liked to sit and talk. While Michael attended to the guests, I excused the children and myself from the table. I couldn't wait to sit under a tree and feel the warm summer breeze on my face. We carried our blueberry pie outside to an oasis of shade. "Why does food taste more delicious when eaten outdoors?" I wondered. I lifted my head and squinted up at the bright blue sky. The lines of a familiar poem came to mind, the last stanza of Stevenson's "Summer Sun":

> *Above the hills, along the blue,*
> *Round the bright air with footing true,*
> *To please the child, to paint the rose,*
> *The gardener of the World, he goes.*

The more carefree days of August were quickly slipping away and September was at our doorstep. I had been planning my second year of home education, scribbling notes while in bed, but I wiped my school slate clean of those thoughts for this Sunday afternoon. Emily was setting up the croquet pins in the grass, so I knew what was coming. Donald took my hand and tugged. "Mom, do you want to play croquet with us? I'm green. Emily's yellow. You can be red again." Croquet was our Sunday game. Outdoors, Donald's sandy hair and frank dark eyes are a striking combination in a lad. Indoors, his hair, like my own, might be called "dirty blond," but in the sunshine it turns to gold.

"Yes, I'll be red again," I said. I followed willingly, making a point to ignore the state of the vegetable garden. It didn't take a close inspection to see that its luscious bounty was ready for more of Emma's and my painstaking preserving. This, too, I erased from my mental "to do" list so that I would not be hindered from savoring the afternoon.

Chapter Two

Ripe Tomatoes

A person can show his religion as much in measuring onions as he can in singing Glory Hallelujah.

A Shaker

Emma's garden was overflowing with a bumper crop of tomatoes. Ripe tomatoes of all sizes filled every spare bowl, bucket, and nook of the kitchen. We skinned, boiled, and strained these "love apples," as they were once called, for most of the morning. Perspiration beaded on our faces as the heat in the kitchen rose. The windows let in too little breeze to cool our brows. Seth and Sarah came to play. I assumed that their shortcut through the woods was fast becoming a distinguishable pathway to our house from the parsonage in the village. I stepped outside, stood on the edge of the porch, and made a firm announcement: "Children, do not come into the kitchen for any reason. If you have to talk to me, do so through the window. Only use the front door to enter the house. Grandma and I cannot have even one fly in this kitchen while we are sterilizing."

"What's sterilizing?" Donald asked.

"We are boiling away the germs from the bottles before we fill them." Perhaps a short lesson on microscopic organisms would be in order once home teaching began.

───✦───

With the last lid screwed on tight, we both stood, hands on hips, admiring the rows of shining red bottles full of the fruits of our industry, and quietly waiting to hear the lids seal with a pop. "Sit down, dear," Emma insisted, pulling out a chair. "We'll wash up after lunch."

"Just a minute," I said, and began opening all the doors to the kitchen, ushering in a draught of welcome air. The air was warm enough not to put our hot bottles in danger of cracking and was a welcome relief to our flushed faces. "I don't think we'll ever get these aprons clean again," I despaired when I finally sat down and folded my hands on my lap.

"I suppose we'll have to demote them; they can be our canning aprons," Emma said.

As if the kitchen hadn't been hot enough, Emma began boiling water for corn on the cob. "Children," she called out the door, "here's some corn for you to husk." Next she sliced some bread and the biggest, reddest tomatoes that had been set aside for our tomato sandwiches. One thick slice made a perfect sandwich. Piling the hot corn, buttered and salted, and the sandwiches on plates, we joined the children outside to eat.

"Nothing is redder than a ripe tomato," I said after a juicy swallow.

"I think the tomato sandwich is my favorite," said Emma.

The sweet corn was juicy, too, and we must have looked a sight with our large juicy bites of both tomatoes and corn and our buttery fingers. "Children, you can wash up at the pump," I told them. As they did, they couldn't resist splashing themselves. Emma and I took pleasure at the scene. "I remember doing the same," I told her.

"Me, too," Emma said, smiling. We sat together, staring out over the apple orchard where the children were headed. They ran through the grass, refreshed by their damp hair and clothes, the boys with sticks in their hands for swords. Emma started one of her chats. "Michael is fond of the country and his new job at the canning factory, isn't he?" she asked casually.

"Yes," I said.

"I love the country, don't you?" she ventured in so easy a manner. It occurred to me that her objective was to find out what I thought about our recent move to Appleton, softened by its preface about Michael. My thoughts leapt to Michael. Not too long ago I had told him that country life was suiting me fine. This, however, was a reappraisal. My first opinion was that we would be regressing by moving from the city to this place where my tireless parents had worked hard on the land and had died so young.

"Yes, Michael does like it here. He finds it a romantic place. I think it's the wide, open spaces. I've seen him stare over the meadows and hills—out to the horizon, the sunrise and sunsets—as if there had never been any sky in the city. His business colleagues in Bridgton ate away at him. Whenever we visited Bob and Dora, he left his problems behind him, but it never crossed my mind that he'd want to move us out here."

Emma had a way of opening me up, but she still wasn't satisfied. "Are you glad?" she asked.

I finally obliged her. "With electricity and bathrooms the country is much more appealing," I answered. "Yes, I am glad. And you are generous to have invited us here," I added politely, placing a hand on her arm.

"Good, good," she said, patting my hand. "I like all the replastering and painting Michael has done. I worried that this old house would soon be falling down around my ears. I truly feel younger since your family came." She stood up and I followed. Together we carried our plates into the kitchen to do the washing up.

The conversation, however, was not yet at a close. It was my turn to fish for a confession. "Doesn't Mr. Fortesque make you feel younger?

How many times has he asked you to marry him?" I am not as clever at prefacing questions, and wasn't as successful at getting an answer. She simply told me what I already knew.

"Mr. Fortesque is a good man and a perfect gentleman but..." She paused while her small smile slowly slid its way up at the corners. "I've outlived three husbands, my dear. Don't you think that's enough for one lifetime?"

"It's what *you* think that matters," I responded, and left it at that.

~~~

"Daddy's home!" Emily called out. She abandoned her pile of paper dolls on the living room floor to meet him at the kitchen door. They shared a greeting. "What did you do today, Emily?" he asked.

"Seth and Sarah came over to play," she said.

Emma and I were in the process of carrying the bottled tomatoes down the cellar stairs.

"What beautiful bottles," Michael said.

"I used to can tomatoes in Bridgeton," I said.

Donald had entered the room and heard my comment. "Yes, Mom, but not this many," he corrected.

"Well, we do have a tourist home to run," I reminded them all, but I was tired and it sounded too much like a complaint. Michael joined us in trudging up and down the stairs to shelve the bottles.

"How about a walk in the cool shade of the cemetery?" he suggested.

"I'd like that," I said, "but I need to get off my feet first."

"Of course," he sympathized. "Under the apple tree?"

I nodded and he got out the picnic blanket from the trunk of the car. We lay back, gazing at the feathered clouds sailing slowly above our heads. Bees were buzzing over the clover, crickets were chirping, and we could hear the children playing Swiss Family Robinson in a distant apple tree.

Michael spoke first. "The clouds never made such interesting shapes in Bridgeton."

"You never looked at the clouds in Bridgeton," I responded.

"You're right," he admitted, and a moment later added, "I only had eyes for you." We laughed. He had a way of softening my emotions. I sighed and relaxed further back against his shoulder.

It was my turn to sympathize. "You canned today, too, didn't you?"

"Yes. Corn."

We continued our peaceful cloud-gazing in companionable silence.

Next thing I knew I was very surprised to find myself waking up from a nap, of all things. Michael was gone. The children were gone. The shade of my tree had become a long shadow. Perhaps I had

been awakened by the sound of Mr. Fortesque's car pulling into the drive. He stays for a couple of days each week to oversee the running of his small canning factory in Appleton. A thought shouted at me, "Supper!" I sprang to my feet—as much as a woman expecting a baby in close to five months can spring—and headed for the kitchen door.

Emma had nearly finished preparing supper. "I made a bowl of cottage cheese. I always set some milk out to curdle the day before I can tomatoes," she said. "We didn't want to wake you." Into the oven went a creamy vegetable cheese pie, dotted with pieces of summer squash, topped with thinly sliced tomato.

"What's that wonderful aroma?" I asked. I spotted her cutting board, green with the remains of chopped herbs. "You used that funny herb from the garden, didn't you? I've been meaning to ask you what it is."

"It's sweet basil, a member of the mint family. An Italian woman gave me some seed when she saw my garden was without it. We always talk herbs and flowers whenever she and her husband visit."

I stood in the doorway between the kitchen and sitting room, peering at the back of Mr. Fortesque's head. He was seated comfortably in his favorite armchair, paper doll in hand. Emily was on the floor at his feet, surrounded by a mess of paper scraps and paper doll clothes. She was changing outfits on her dolls and smiling up at him. Once she gets a certain plaything set up, she continues with it for a good many days with a persevering interest. Emily saw me watching her in the doorway and briefly lifted up a doll so I could admire the newest dress. "That's a colorful one," I commented, for lack of a better adjective. I was distracted by the catchy tune Mr. Fortesque's was humming. It sounded so familiar. "What *is* that song?" I wondered.

I set the table and soon we were all sitting around it. Mr. Fortesque was our only guest. He always seemed to lend a certain luster to our evenings. He was his jolly self, sharing anecdotes and asking the children questions. He relished his food. "Nourishing country bounty," he called it, composing a string of other flamboyant compliments to the cook through his out-of-date handlebar mustache, which he frequently wiped clean with his napkin. Not a crumb was left on his

plate. This time, however, he very oddly turned down a second helping of cheese pie and passed on a bowl of blackberry cobbler. This
was not the usual way of this portly gentleman.

After supper Mr. Fortesque went out to the garden "for a think,"
as he put it. I washed the dishes and Michael dried. As I stood at the
sink I spied, through the window, Mr. Fortesque hiking up the little
hill of the cemetery and then trudging all around the periphery of
the apple orchard.

"It isn't normal for Mr. Fortesque to take walks, is it?" I noted.

"We haven't known him long enough to know what's normal,"
Michael answered. "But come to think of it, he usually relaxes after
supper with a pipe or cigar."

"That's what I thought," I said.

"He probably has business on his mind, Carol. He's a man of
much responsibility," he said soberly.

But his mood changed abruptly when I asked, "Michael, what's
this song?" I gave it the best la-la-la that I could, not knowing the
words.

"Why?" he asked, chuckling.

"Mr. Fortesque was humming the tune earlier."

"Sure, I know that one." Then he started singing it, stepping to
the beat as he put the dishes away. "I'm gonna buy a paper doll that
I can call my own..."

My private thought was, "How interesting."

Chapter Three

Dora's Invitation

*Beauty is God's
handwriting.
Welcome it in
every fair face,
every fair day,
every fair flower.*
Charles Kingsley

For as long as I could remember the church people had come together for a picnic on Labor Day, but this year's bounty required all hands and all spare hours for harvesting and so, well in advance, the picnic was called off. Michael and Donald left early in their overalls to help Bob with harvesting. Michael would return with the car just before midday to pick up Emily and me, for the day of our tea with Dora had arrived. Emma offered to attend to Blackberry Inn's weekend guests, urging Emily and me to leave her to it. Geraldine came to do the washing and ironing. I was so thankful to have her, and she was thankful for my automatic washing machine with wringer attached.

"It is a good thing I'm driving you," said Michael. "Otherwise you would have a windy walk."

"Yes, it is rather breezy, isn't it?" I said.

"See you later," he said, and was off with Donald.

I was glad we would be chauffeured because I had set Emily's honey-colored hair in rag curls the night before. I wanted to hold some shape to the ragging efforts of my own hair, too, since it had grown to my shoulders. From Blackberry Inn Bob and Dora's farm is a three-and-a-half-mile walk. They live north of the village. We live south of it. I'd enjoy popping in to see Dora less formally and more often if we lived closer. Emily and I dusted the big house together, which is no small chore, and then dressed in our best.

"That's a pretty dress," Emma told Emily. "Take these with you." She handed Emily a small bouquet of her late-blooming roses, bound at the stems with a tight wrapping of brown paper for safe handling. "It's proper to bring flowers or another small gift when you're invited to tea."

Emily clasped the bouquet, holding it with the utmost of care, as if it were made of glass crystal. "Thank you, Grandma." Upon hearing Emma's reminder I tied some purple calico to the lid of a jar of black-berry preserves. Then we waited for Michael, seated primly (Emily bolt upright) in the sitting room.

~⌒⌒~

I enjoyed the drive. Signs of September were everywhere. A squir-rel was hurriedly burying a nut with rapid strokes of his paws. In front of the village houses the strong breeze shook crab apples off the trees. The marble-sized apples dropped along the lane. In back gardens wheelbarrows were being filled with vegetables for the root cellar. When we pulled into my parents' old farm, Dora's orange mari-golds—overflowing their clay pots—caught my eye. It is always pleas-ing to anticipate annuals reaching their peak when the perennials are looking spent.

Upon getting out of the car, I scanned the farm further, noticing the perennials which had been there since my childhood, especially the tall phlox. They had grown and spread to big clumps. Apparently, hovering about my sister-in-law is a certain whimsical romanticism, for Dora let knee-deep perennials spring up where one would never suppose they belonged. It comforted me to take a good long look at the one-and-a-half story house I had been raised in. Even weathered white clapboard is bright against a sky as blue as the chicory in the pasture.

Michael returned to the field, and Emily and I entered the house by the front door. "Come in, come in, ladies," greeted Dora, baby Jonathan balanced on her hip. My seven-month-old nephew was as big and plump as a plum pudding. It didn't seem long ago when, as a newborn, his tiny head fit in my hand and the rest of his body could be cradled in one arm. "Let me show you into the parlor while I put the baby down for his nap. Are these for me? Oh, how beautiful. I love bicolor roses. I'll be right back." Dora's eyes are large and her complexion rosy. Her long chestnut hair is always neatly braided and crossed over her head like a crown, but that day she had baby's-breath tucked into it, resembling that of a bridesmaid.

Emily and I sat primly once more, Emily taking in the table, which had been set with Dora's best china. She counted the place settings. There were five. "Who else is coming?" she asked observantly.

"I'm interested to find out," I said. "Have you ever seen such tiny sandwiches?"

"The pickles are little, too," she noted.

"Oh, yes, sweet gherkins, mmm."

I could hear Dora in the kitchen running water for tea and for the roses. The moment she entered the parlor with her vase, there was a knock on the door and she was off again. A minute later Sarah entered the room. Both girls were instantly all smiles and Emily's straight back relaxed. Sarah's mother entered just behind her daughter. Penelope is Pastor Bingham's wife. She is a woman who, for the sake of prayer, minds more than her own business, yet involves herself in the affairs of others only when it is welcomed. She is a thin and somewhat faded-looking woman; today, however, her salt and pepper hair was less plain. When she removed her kerchief, I noticed her low bun was looser and had ringlets around it. Being windblown made it more becoming. Her lavender dress, probably reserved for all her Easter Sundays, gave her a brighter air.

Dora tried to put us at ease. "I hope you don't feel any shame in enjoying a brief restorative while the men folk are bringing in the sheaves, so to speak."

Penelope spoke with her usual directness. "Your invitation helped me get through many hours of preserving. Just knowing I had something so pleasant to look forward to made my work lighter. No Dora, I don't feel any shame." After a prayer of blessing, Dora filled the girls' teacups with mostly milk, then a spot of black tea from my mother's blue and white teapot. Her well-bred manners comfortably included the girls in our conversation, but they eventually settled into the giggles of their own private prattle. Dora served the finger sandwiches that we barely needed to open our mouths for, then we all sampled each dainty dessert. "May I have your recipe for this lemon cake?" I asked, as I rose to help clear away the things.

"The cake is Emma's recipe," she said. "And the gherkins are Penelope's pickling. I was saving them for just the right occasion." I was being welcomed into a circle of friends.

At the mention of Emma, Penelope asked me, "How do you like it at Emma's house?"

"It's working out well," I answered. "I've always admired Emma."

"She and your mother were quite close for years, weren't they?"

"Yes, quite close," I said.

Emily was squirming, so I whispered in her ear, "You may ask Dora to be excused if you have to use the necessary." She asked, and so did Sarah. Together they flitted off in their ruffled dresses like fairies set free, except for the banging of the screen door behind them.

I insisted on doing the washing up while Dora brought a large sewing basket to the oft-used, oft-scrubbed kitchen table, much the contrast to our parlor seating. "Here's what I wanted to show you. It's all the rage for using up small fabric pieces. They're called yo-yos."

"Where did you hear about these?" Penelope asked.

"In this issue of *Mothers' Companion*," she said. She pulled the magazine from her basket and held it open. Pressing an index finger under a passage, she read aloud. "'I think a genuine love of the beautiful is innate in the heart of every girl and woman.'" Then she looked up at us and asked, "Don't you agree?"

"Oh yes, and these yo-yos are darling. Come and look at this, girls," Penelope said when they returned. It was the first time I had seen Penelope's countenance so bright. She shared, "I've never forgotten the recommendation of artist William Morris since I first read of it. I've dreamed of one day putting up one of his leafy wallpaper designs in our parlor."

"His recommendation?" asked Dora.

"Yes, it's his motto. He said to have nothing in your house that you do not know to be useful, or believe to be beautiful."

"Hmm, I like that," said Dora giving it some thought.

Penelope confessed slight disappointment. "I keep his motto in the back of my mind, but I haven't been able to fully accomplish it. *Mud*, for one, demands constant vigilance."

Dora conceded wholeheartedly, "Oh, I agree." *Manure* is what I was thinking, what we were all thinking, but none of us dared to mention it.

While I was at the sink I listened to Dora's instructions for making yo-yos out of cotton calico scraps. She guided us through the steps of cutting a circle, sewing a running stitch around its hem, and gathering the circle up and securing it with a knot. She then unfolded a small table coverlet she had made with a collection of yo-yos sewn together at the edges. "You can make matching pillows, too, or even an entire bedspread. But you'll need hundreds of yo-yos for that." Making a yo-yo was a craft that amiably accommodated the needle skills of both Emily and Sarah. Penelope was thoroughly enjoying herself when I joined them. Her creative imagination had been warmed up. She said gaily, "I think I might have enough red and green fabric scraps at home to make a pillow cover for Christmas."

When Jonathan awoke from his nap, Penelope said, "We must be off. Thank you for a lovely time." After a pause she shared more intimately. "I don't know how to tell you how good it feels to be ministered to." Her eyes turned moist at the sentiment, but she kept them from dropping any tears while she and Sarah were seen to the front door and given one of Dora's farewell hugs. She was departing for home with peace of mind and body restored. A country mother has very little time for herself, especially a pastor's wife. Penelope gives unselfishly to her husband and six children with as much taking care as is needed, and there is indeed much taking care for a country wife and mother. I thought, "True love pours itself out like a drink offering," to quote St. Paul. Recently Penelope and Pastor had driven their three eldest sons to the train station in Forest Green. Two sons had set off for college, one for seminary. Emma had confided in me that she suspected that all and any funds that came into the church for Pastor's salary were set apart for college. Like the majority of the congregation, the Binghams scraped a living almost entirely from the land. Perhaps their parting had been fresh in Penelope's thoughts.

With the tea party coming to a close, my mind ran ahead to tomorrow's first day of home teaching. I wondered if either of my children—but especially Emily—would pout about not attending the village school where they would be sure to see their friends every day. Would this separation seem a punishment of sorts?

While Dora nursed the baby in private, Emily and I sat close, making more yo-yos from different colors of fabric. "Lessons start tomorrow," I told her with a positive ring in my voice.

"Yes, I know, Mommy. Sarah is starting school tomorrow, too."

Dora entered the kitchen carrying Jonathan. "Emily, would you like to play with Jonathan?" she asked. "Let's go back into the parlor."

"Okay," she said. "He's getting cuter."

"Here you go." Dora set them up on a blanket on the parlor floor, although she knew Jonathan would soon be creeping beyond its bounds. Next she turned to me, as we sat together on the sofa. "How are things at Emma's house?" Feeling uncomfortable, and beginning to figure out why, I thought, "There's that phrase again—*Emma's house.*" I was more than uncomfortable. I was dazed and disgruntled.

"Carol?"

I collected myself. "Oh, yes, we're happy to have Emma as the children's newly adopted grandmother since Michael's parents are back in Wales, and my parents are gone from us. Michael is happy, the children love it here, and I'm feeling better. How are you? It was so kind of you to have us for tea."

"To be honest, I've been lonely for a bit of society," she said. "It's good seeing you again."

I desired to be consoling to my young and pretty sister-in-law, who was still getting used to country life. "It's a busy time of year. Neighbors have far less time to stop and chat at the general store. I'm looking forward to the Apple Butter Festival, aren't you? How about coming for supper sometime when we have guests. Would you like that?"

"I'd like that very much," she said. "I'll move the soup back to the front burner for the men. They've built up an appetite by now, no doubt."

"No doubt," I echoed.

Chapter Four

A Well-Stocked Library

*If you have
a garden and
a library you
have everything
you need.*

Cicero

Emily, at eight years of age, and Donald, at ten, seemed to be looking forward to their first day of being home taught. I prayed that if they were in any way disappointed that they were not attending the village school, where they would have seen Seth and Sarah every day, that I could make up for this somehow.

I was poised to begin Picture Study, something I hadn't yet tried during our first year of home education. The previous school year I had thought it wise to give myself time to settle in to what I was gleaning from my trusty book, *Home Education*, by Miss Charlotte Mason. It was a happy circumstance for me when I received this book as a present from Michael's sister, who lives in Wales. It was becoming increasingly more valuable to me. I had tried putting into practice a little at a time what I was reading in it.

This year I was ready to try Picture Study, and in fact was looking forward to it. The oversized book of art prints in Emma's well-stocked library was a wonderful resource to be in possession of—even if it did not strictly follow Miss Mason's sensible recommendation to become familiar with the works and style of one artist at a time. If I followed her plan exactly, I would display at least six of one artist's work during one semester. If I could make arrangements, however, for a collection of pictures to be mailed to me, our tight budget would most likely only allow for postcard-size black and whites. "Make do" is what we did during the Depression years, and Emma's copy of *Famous Paintings— Selected from the World's Great Galleries and Reproduced in Colour*, with descriptive notes by G.K. Chesterton, was very welcome to me. Rather than go in page order, during my weeks of bed rest I had bookmarked pictures that I had thought were best suited to the younger ages.

Like a parent secretly setting out gifts the night before Christmas, I had set out my materials in the library the night before lessons. "The Angelus," by the French artist Jean François Millet, would be the first thing to catch the eyes of my children. Millet was cited as an example in *Home Education* and successfully appreciated by the students in Miss Mason's schools. G. K. Chesterton's notes about the painting were a pleasure to read during my bed rest. His insights revealed him to be a lover of art. He wrote that Millet's paintings depicted peasants true to life "with the symbolical dignity of labor." In "The Angelus," the laborers stop and give thanks to God for the gift of plenty. His notes were all I would need to maintain my own enthusiasm for art throughout the year and give the children a little background and explanation that would not interfere with their own observations.

Over the months I would listen to the children take turns narrating their observations of many of the wonderful pictures in Emma's book. But on that morning, aside from displaying Millet's picture, I only told them a little about the artist. I asked no questions, nor did I require them just yet to narrate what they saw. They were only to look, and to look closely.

Speaking of narration, this was something Donald and Emily hadn't done all summer. To ease them into the close attention required for putting the reading into their own words, I chose an American Indian tale from *My Book House*. Today Emily seemed a bit rusty at narrating. While she retold the tale, I had to place a finger over my lips, a signal to Donald not to interrupt, because Emily's words came out slowly. Narration is work. I trusted that this skill would continue to develop as my children were educated by good books and experiences.

Another of Emma's books (this one I had found in her attic) looked like just the thing for reading aloud and narrating, and Donald proved this to be true. It is an early American history book from 1903 that has an emphasis on biography. Its preface claims that "the telling of history in stories of the lives of its makers has a quality of concreteness very attractive to children, who usually fail to be interested in chronological narratives of events wherein the personal element is less prominent." The author of this book and Charlotte Mason are in agreement. Miss Mason recommended a *story style* of history that with vivid descriptive power presented a shorter time period as well as the "people aspect." She said that such books

> *are just the thing for the children whose eager souls want
> to get at the living people behind the words of the history
> book, caring nothing at all about progress, or statures, or
> about anything but the persons, for whose action history
> is, to the child's mind, no more than a convenient stage. A
> child who has been carried through a single [history] in
> this way has a better foundation for an historical training
> than if he knew all the dates and names and facts that
> ever were crammed for examination.*

With this as their foundation, years later we may "put any dull outlines into their hands and they will make history for themselves," she wrote.

Most of my children's oral narration would come from history. I was glad that our chapters were short enough for even Emily. I would assign Donald a lengthier biography or two for his silent reading. I expected the children to keep a notebook of key passages from their history narration, together with drawings. My decision was based, again, on what Miss Mason had written:

> *History readings afford admirable material for narration, and the children enjoy narrating what they read or have heard. They love, too, to make illustrations. Children who had been reading Julius Caesar...were asked to make a picture of their favorite scene, and the results showed the extraordinary power of visualizing which the little people possess. Of course that which they visualize, or imagine clearly, they know; it is a life possession.*

Since we were without our new arithmetic books, as they were still on order, I gave the children some mental arithmetic as a refresher. Scanning an old copy of *Brooks' Mental Arithmetic* gave me the idea, but I had to make up my own arithmetic situations. The ones in *Brooks* were stale and unimaginative. Donald and Emily first took turns translating my arithmetic stories into equations on the chalkboard easel, and then doing some in their head. I tried to create situations that were adventurous, like those strange adventures they met up with in *Swiss Family Robinson*—a story they knew well. I was surprised to hear Donald say, "Can I make one up now, Mom?"

"*May* I make one up?" I corrected. "Yes you may, but keep it simple. Emily and I aren't ready to be too challenged yet," I said, knowing his desire to embellish.

Henry Wadsworth Longfellow was to be one of our poets. He was my father's favorite. A book from my brother Bob's shelf promised to supply us with plenty of Longfellow poems. On that morning I started reading aloud "Hiawatha's Fasting," a legend of the first Indian corn. It is included in Dad's book, but *My Book House* includes it, too, with illustrations. For Emily's sake I would also read from a children's anthology a variety of shorter poems during the year to supply material for her copy work, which Miss Mason called transcription. In *Home Education* she wrote:

The earliest practice in writing for children of seven or eight should be, not letter writing or dictation, but transcription, slow and beautiful work...Transcription should be an introduction to spelling. Children should be encouraged to look at the word, see a picture of it with their eyes shut, and then write [it] from memory...A book of their own made up of their own chosen verses should give them pleasure.

With the kitchen cleared of Geraldine's ironing and lunch over, I knocked on Emma's door. Her bedroom is on the far side of the kitchen, just past the pantry and new first-floor bathroom. It overlooks the kitchen garden, which is so close to the house that the scent of herbs wafts in through her windows whenever there is a sturdy breeze.

"Come in," she said.

I poked my head in the door. "I hope I'm not disturbing you. Do you have a minute?"

"Come in, dear," she said, peeking over her reading glasses at me. She was sitting at the desk of her secretary near the window with a letter in her hand. "Doesn't the breeze smell lovely? Something other than onions," she added, taking off her glasses.

"Yes, I guessed you'd strung up the onions when I passed the cellar door just now," I said.

Inside the secretary were small photos in frames. A locket on a necklace lay open on the desk. I had never seen her wear it.

She asked, "How did your lessons go?"

"Very well. It was an introduction really. Some of the children's excitement today is their anticipation of the chickens. Bob's bringing them over later because Michael and Donald are finally finished with the coop. Is it okay to pick the green tomatoes and pull up their roots? I think Donald should bring in the butternut squash to the cellar, don't you? I fear a frost coming."

"Yes, frost is on the way, near but not imminent." Emma liked to putter around her garden and let the soles of her bare feet warn her of frost.

I stepped closer to the secretary and stood alongside her. My eye was on the tiny locket. "That's a lovely locket," I hazarded.

"It's a photo of Dr. Cook," she volunteered, sensing my curiosity. "I'm starting a letter to my daughter in Oregon, the daughter of my second husband. This is her picture." She lifted it up for me to hold.

"She has your smile. But I thought she lived in Kansas."

"She did, but because of drought they had to sell up and move further west."

I had difficulty conceptualizing how very far away Oregon was and felt sad for her. Because her daughter was now even farther away, what chance had she of ever seeing her daughter or grandchildren? Placing the picture back on the secretary, I leaned forward to get a closer look at the locket. "My, Dr. Cook sure was handsome," I said.

"Yes," she said, "he was handsome in so many ways, my dear." Cupping the open locket in her hands, she held her gaze upon it for a moment, then fastened it closed and tucked it into its special spot in her desk with a fluid dexterity, indicating that she had probably done so many times. "It's been five years."

"I'm sorry I never got to meet him," I said.

"I am, too," she said.

"I'll start supper as soon as I'm through tidying the tomato plants."

"Thank you, dear. I'll make a big batch of my green tomato relish first thing in the morning." And she picked up her pen, preparing to dip it in the ink.

I worked in the garden just below Emma's window. When I had nearly finished, I felt an arm around my back. It was Michael's warm hello.

"Oh, you startled me!" I exclaimed. I was on my knees with my hands in the soil. Emma's garden was not an ordinary garden of rows. It was somewhat wildly established in clumps alongside garden paths, vegetables with flowers, flowers with herbs, more herbs around the birdbath. Wild things obeyed her. Though she interrupted their freedom, only seldom did she stake, trim, or rearrange. Her art of gardening was a mystery to me. While growing up I had paid little attention to my mother's similar powers.

"How's my country girl?" Michael asked in greeting.

"Good," I said. He scanned the distant orchard and closer by where his newly finished coop stood. He looked satisfied. "How was work?" I asked.

"Stuffy," he said. His chest expanded as he inhaled deeply. After a long breath he said, "Mmm, fresh air. You know, Carol, I feel so at home here with you," he commented as he exhaled. I smiled, grabbed hold of a tomato plant, and shook the soil off it. Then I wiped away the grains that hit my face with the back of a gloved hand. When I stood up and placed the plant on top of my pile in the wheelbarrow, he took both my garden-gloved hands in his and asked, "Do you feel at home, Carol?"

Perplexed, I didn't want to answer. I averted his dark, entreating eyes. "Carol," he persisted, "your feelings are important to me."

I asked a stupid question, "Honestly?"

"Honestly."

"I don't feel quite at home yet, Michael. Sometimes I feel like..." I turned away.

He waited patiently while I kneeled down to pull up the last tomato plant by the roots. When I stood up, he said, "You feel like what?"

"Like only a caretaker of Emma's house. In fact that's what everyone calls it, *Emma's house.*" I gave my plant a fast pitch into the wheelbarrow. "I know we invested all our savings into this house for its renovation but after all, it won't be our house until Emma leaves this earth and we inherit it." Though my words were not harshly spoken, they sounded dreadful to me.

"I think she'd like us to think of it as our house, too, *right now.*"

"Yes, Michael. I believe so. She *is* a most gracious, most generous, easy-to-get-along-with woman, a woman who is lonely for family. I *am* happy that she has adopted us as her family."

"I am, too," Michael said, and he said nothing else. He meant to listen, that is all. He gave me one of his hugs without words. Then he took hold of the wheelbarrow full of tomato plants and strode away with it across the garden to dump it for me.

⁓

Later that evening Bob arrived and unpacked his truck of the chickens, poured us out some milk, and gave us a gift of a half-bushel of ripe tomatoes. "We've a bumper crop this year," he said.

"Thank you," I told him, and refrained from adding, "so have we."

Dora winked at me knowingly, and said, "You have your work cut out for you." We all congregated at the coop. Dora initiated the idea of thinking up names for each hen and ways to identify it by its slight peculiarities. Emma stood beside the children, greatly amused by the names.

Evidently, the chickens had done enough scratching for one day and climbed inside the coop. "They always get sleepy near sunset," Emma told them. Then she bid us follow her into the kitchen for her coconut oatmeal cookies.

～⌒～

When the house was quiet and all were in bed, I crept downstairs to the library. In order to sleep soundly I needed to take a few minutes to set straight in my mind what the following day's lessons would entail. A book needed straightening on the bookshelf. Before pushing it back in line with the others, I was curious to know the title. The bookmark itself was provocative, its purple glass bead resting above a dangling tassel. It was a poetry book of Emma's. She must have just finished reading it. I pulled it out, and opening it up to where it was marked, I read the poem, "Home."

> *It takes a heap o' livin' in a house t' make it home,...*

The topic led me to believe that Emma had left her book askew intentionally. Michael and I had been talking just below her window, and she could still have been in her bedroom, writing. Emma was not one to listen at keyholes, but she probably couldn't help overhear our conversation. By her standards it wouldn't be fitting to lecture me. She wouldn't even leave the book out on the library table. No, Emma's tactics were subtle. I was touched by the sentiment of the poem and would even read it again, secretly. But I wouldn't go so far as to say I was appreciative. In fact I was too embarrassed to let her know that she had overheard us—even if she had chosen the poem for my benefit. No, I would leave the book just as I found it. I couldn't cope with her knowing I'd read it. Not yet, anyway.

Home

By Edgar A. Guest (1881-1959)

It takes a heap o' livin' in a house t' make it home,
A heap o' sun an' shadder, an' ye sometimes have t' roam
Afore ye really 'preciate the things ye lef' behind,
An' hunger fer 'em somehow, with 'em allus on yer mind.
It don't make any differunce how rich ye get t' be,
How much yer tables an' chairs cost, how great yer luxury;
It ain't home t' ye, though it be the palace of a king,
Until somehow yer soul is sort o' wrapped 'round everything.

Home ain't a place that gold can buy or get up in a minute;
Afore it's home there's got t' be a heap o' livin' in it;
Within the walls there's got t' be some babies born, and then
Right there you've got t' bring 'em up t' women good an' men;
And gradjerly, as time goes on, ye find ye wouldn't part
With anything they ever used—they've grown into yer heart:
The old high chairs, the playthings, too, the little shoes they wore
Ye hoard; an' if ye could ye'd keep the thumb-marks on the door.

Ye've got t' weep t' make it a home, ye've got t' sit an' sigh
An' watch beside a loved one's bed, an' know that Death is nigh;
An' in the stillness o' the night t' see Death's angel come,
An' close the eyes o' her that smiled, an' leave her sweet voice dumb.
Fer these are scenes that grip the heart, an' when yer tears are dried,
Ye find the home is dearer than it was, an' sanctified;
An' tuggin' at ye always are the pleasant memories
Of her that was an' is no more—ye can't escape from these.

Ye've got to sing an' dance fer years, ye've got to romp an' play,
An' learn to love the things ye have by usin' 'em each day;
Even the rose 'round the porch must blossom year by year
Afore they 'come apart o' ye, suggestin' someone dear
Who used t' love 'em long ago, and trained 'em just t' run
The way they do, so's they would get the early mornin' sun;
Ye've got to love each brick an' stone from cellar up to dome:
It takes a heap o' livin' in a house t' make it home.

Chapter Five

Trusting Character

*The highest
reward for a
person's toil is not
what they get for
it, but what they
become by it.*

John Ruskin

During our morning lessons the children used dominoes to practice arithmetic. We covered the table with dominoes, facedown. Taking turns, they picked one and read the sum of the sides. As they played they increased their speed. For the next round of dominoes I had the children pick four, write their sums in a column, and get the sum of these. To simplify, I showed them how to make tens to get a faster total. We played two more games then got on with our other subjects, moving into the sitting room for history.

With Geraldine's newly-ironed sheets, Emily and I made the guest beds and Donald went over the floors with the dust mop. He is my floor boy, sweeping the stairs and the kitchen floor, though he needs to get better at cleaning corners. Geraldine, who is French, teaches Donald and Emily three new words at the beginning of each week when she comes to do the washing and ironing. I especially like how she speaks French to them in short conversational sentences. She is a double blessing to me.

It was fair weather, and after we were released from our chores, the children and I walked to the village. I bought the beef bones I had ordered from the butcher, pocketing two pennies. Just as we were leaving the butcher shop, the children of Appleton poured through the door of the schoolhouse into the sunshine. Donald and Emily ran over to their friends while I stepped into the general store. Eyeing some yarn of a beautiful shade of red that would be just right for mittens, I resolved to keep saving pennies.

"Let's go, children," I called, and we walked home along Paw Print Road.

Donald said, "Seth asked what we did today, and I told him we played dominoes for lessons."

I could already hear it going around the village that the Weaver children played games instead of doing schoolwork. "Did you tell him it was our way of remembering our facts?" I said in mild consternation.

"I think so," he said.

"Never mind," I said. "This is perfect weather for walking, and it has been ages since I've walked with you." I was remembering our previous year's Nature Study and how refreshing and educational our walks had been. A flock of swallows flew overhead. "I always feel sad when the swallows leave," I said.

The countryside's white doilies of Queen Anne's lace had dried into their tight shapes. "Look at all the birds' nests," said Emily. It was our name for these dried flowers.

"Here's some Jerusalem artichoke, right, Mom?" Donald spotted a tuft of tired-looking golden daisies against a fence post. Emily tried picking some, but their stems were so sinewy that Donald had to use his penknife on them.

"These daisies have tubers like potatoes and, like potatoes, they are edible," I said.

"Should I pull up the roots, Mom?" Donald asked.

"Let's leave the artichokes for someone else," I said, not wishing to deal with them. And we strolled along, talking about the natural world around us.

～～

Moments after we returned I had the beef bones simmering. I was making vegetable beef soup. Though the amount of beef in the soup was minimal, I knew that the broth from the bones was good for us.

Soon afterwards Emily and I had the kitchen table covered with calico fabric scraps and were cutting out circles for our yo-yos. It felt good to sit down. Emma had been out back much of the day saving seeds and drying them in the sun. She had gathered herbs and tied them in bundles for drying. "Some of those herbs could hang near your wide fireplace. They would add a nice early American ambiance to the sitting room," I told her, mindful of the history the children and I were studying, I suppose.

"Yes, dear, you're right," she said, happy I was showing an interest. When Emma noticed our circle cutting, she was curious. I let Emily tell her grandmother about what she and Sarah had learned at the tea party. Then when Emma stepped outside again through the kitchen door, I whispered in Emily's ear, "Shall we make a yo-yo pillow for Grandma?" She liked the idea. I was thinking ahead of Christmas, but didn't say so. "It will be our secret," I told her, and we began picking colors with Grandma in mind.

Emma must have seen the cars pull into the drive. Within minutes, she came inside, crossed the kitchen, and stood looking through the entrance to the sitting room. It sounded like Michael and Mr. Fortesque were already through the front door, talking as they came. From the edge of the sitting room, Emma sang out her usual, "Coffee with cream, gentlemen?"

"Yes, thank you," Michael said.

"None for me, thank you. Some of that cold well water, please, Mrs. Cook," requested Mr. Fortesque.

"Don't go out of your way making coffee just for me; I'll have water, too, please," Michael amended.

"That's odd," Emma mumbled, stepping up to the cupboard for glasses.

"What's odd?" I asked, without looking up from my cutting. But she didn't answer. She was busy filling the glasses with water.

~~~

As it was not the weekend yet, Mr. Fortesque was once again the only guest at our supper table. "This is the most wholesome nourishment I've eaten all week. Such a kaleidoscope of vegetables in this soup," Mr. Fortesque praised. And so creatively, too. But his appetite was not the same, as he turned down a piece of Emma's vanilla cake with coconut frosting. And he seemed a little less gregarious at the table that evening. Emma's face expressed quiet concern. When Donald asked if Mr. Fortesque wanted to see our new hens, he followed the children outside. Afterwards he took another of his long solitary walks.

When the children returned, I told them to go upstairs and get ready for bed. "Because we're going to start our new story," I announced. We had finished *Heidi*.

"What are we going to read next?" Donald asked.

"I'm not telling," I said. In *Home Education* Miss Mason has much practical advice on the use of habit. Stipulation and a little suspense have their uses, too, I had discovered. It also kept my children from needing constant prodding. They could look forward to story time only after teeth were brushed, pajamas were on, and any toys were picked up. A new story was an even greater motivation. Moments later, I passed the men in the living room and walked into the library for *Black Beauty*. My attention was drawn to the spot on the bookshelf where I had found Emma's poetry book. It had been pushed back into place. I was a little unnerved.

Suddenly Michael appeared in the doorway of the library. "Carol, come sit with us a minute. I have interesting news."

"Really?" I said. Together we seated ourselves across from his boss. "Mr. Fortesque says we ought to have a telephone." My first thought was how would we afford it. Besides the canning factory, in our sleepy village only the general store and the doctor had a telephone. When an important call came for Pastor it came to the general store and its owner walked next door to the parsonage to get him.

Mr. Fortesque explained. "For several weeks I will be out of state, and will need to contact Michael after business hours. The bill will come here, but the canning factory will pay for it."

"And we'll be able to receive telephone inquires for Blackberry Inn, so now I can advertise properly," Michael said.

I didn't know what to say. To fill the silence, Mr. Fortesque praised Michael's administrative skills. At this Michael's response was, "I still

don't know why you hired me in the first place; I knew nothing about canning factories, even a small one such as yours."

"Michael is being too modest," I thought. He had learned very recently that he was replacing a man who had been dismissed for negligence, a man who proved hostile to receiving instruction if it meant correction or improvement.

Mr. Fortesque replied, "Mrs. Cook knows people. If she liked you enough to trust you with her house, and adopt you as her family, I knew I could trust you to work out my list of instructions without prior experience. Give me a man of character and the rest falls into place."

"In your absence, trial and error helped me figure out what *wasn't* on your list," Michael confessed, leaning back into the cushions and smiling, his pipe held firmly between his lips.

Mr. Fortesque threw his head back and gave a loud "Hah!" There was something so genuine in his laugh, in his utter rejection of the idea that Michael was not fit for the position, that his sincerity could not be questioned. He gave a series of puffs on his pipe and then said, "It isn't smooth sailing that makes a good mariner. The fact that you admit to using trial and error proves you're an honest man. And honesty is not a wee thing. You wouldn't play their game at your old firm, Michael, and that's why they had to get rid of you. I know those unscrupulous men—your employers. I know them by name."

Michael removed his pipe from his mouth and leaned forward. "You do?"

Frowning, Mr. Fortesque continued, "A man who underhandedly hides his mistakes or blames his underlings is both a shyster *and* a wimp." This Scotsman was just as free in his appraisal of character as he was with the supper menu.

Michael pondered aloud, "So you know my old employers."

"Aye."

"Well, I'm glad it all happened, because we ended up here."

"It's good for the bairns," said Mr. Fortesque nodding at me. "I like it here, too; I crave the peace of it." Puffing at his pipe more sedately from the side of his mouth, he added, "But business in town keeps me away. I can't separate myself from the city just yet." I felt for this man who kept his eggs in many baskets. I noticed that his suit, which had always fit him like a glove, had become somehow misshapen. Here was a bachelor in need of a suit that was not as out-of-style as his large moustache—a red moustache that had gained a few more white hairs of late.

I excused myself politely and climbed the long stairs with my book. I looked forward to this cozy hour of bedtime reading at the close of the day, perhaps as much as the children. They instantly became fond of the horse, Black Beauty, and I enjoyed Anna Sewell's colorful writing. Half a chapter of reading was plenty for one night. I closed the book, tucked them in, and kissed my "bairns" good night.

Michael was already in our bedroom when I flopped down into one of our easy chairs and removed the shoes from my aching feet. I decided I might as well bring up the subject of going to Bridgeton for the arithmetic books and for new shoes for the children, while it was fresh on my mind. "...and so, Michael, why don't we go this Saturday?" I finished.

"If we go, it will be just the two of us."

I blinked my eyes. "What did you say?"

"We haven't been alone together since...you know, I can't remember," he said, turning his gaze to the window to think about it.

"But I always buy the children new shoes this time of year," I protested. "They'll need to be there to be fitted."

"It can wait," he said, returning his gaze to me. "Anyway I think we ought to get *you* shoes with my next paycheck," he said.

"Me?"

"Look at yourself," he said. "You're rubbing your feet. I've caught you in the act. Wouldn't you like a new pair of shoes?"

"Well, yes, but..."

"I'd like *very* much to buy you a pair this Saturday," he stated. When Michael's mind is made up, it remains made up, especially when presented with my weak arguments. He never imposes his will, but his kind diplomacy makes me want to obey him.

"I'll pack a picnic lunch and we'll eat in the park and make a day of it," I said, getting excited about the idea.

"It's a deal," he said, smiling. "Now how about getting ready for bed, my girl?"

I had almost fallen asleep, but he started talking again. "Carol?" he asked serenely.

"Hmm?"

"Do you know what makes me the most happy about our getting a telephone?"

"What?" I responded, yawning.

"When you're ready to have the baby, we can call the doctor straight away."

"That's nice," I said, and felt comfortably free from all care beside him.

Chapter Six

The Alley Door

Eden is that
  old-fashioned house
We dwell in every day
Without suspecting
  our abode
Until we drive away.
Emily Dickinson,
No. 1657 (N.D.), ST. I

Saturday morning I awoke to the tweets of my loyal pair of cardinals. Whoever invented the English word *tweet* must have derived it from this bird. Its call is the epitome of tweet.

"Michael, I didn't know my cardinals were parents."

"*Your* cardinals?" he said, joining me at the window. I held aside the curtain and together we watched the family of birds directly below us. The female was pecking at the edge of the bushes. The male was pecking and scavenging, too, but was being followed into the bushes by two fat, overgrown fledglings. The fledglings shook their feathers, crying tweeting cries, trying the father's patience, wanting to be spoon-fed as they had been in their days in the nest.

"I've never seen that before," Michael said.

"Me, either," I said.

"The red one is the male, right? Why is he still feeding them? They're fatter than *he* is." Both parents looked thin and scruffy, but the male appeared to be the more worn out of the two. A nearby robin, standing in the grass, was far more robust. We could just make out the scene in all the fog. It seemed that Keats' "season of mist and mellow fruitfulness" was upon us.

"I hope the fog lifts," I said.

"Me, too," he returned.

On Friday, the day previous, Emily—when she heard that her dad and I were having a picnic—had told me that she wanted to have a picnic, too, so we worked together to prepare food for our baskets. She and Donald would walk to the parsonage to meet up with Seth and Sarah and then decide where to picnic. Emma planned to go in the opposite direction on her bicycle. She would visit her friends, the Goslin sisters, who hadn't been in church for weeks.

"I hope the children will be all right while we're gone," I said.

"Don't worry, Emma will be here most of the day."

"Right," I said, and finished dressing, wondering how my curls could possibly last the day in all the fog.

Appleton's roads were wet and bumpy but we soon reached the main road heading east. It had been two whole months since I had last been in Bridgeton—the day we had moved from there to Appleton. I remember Michael's eagerness to go where "the sunset is not wasted on roof lines," and where a man isn't pushed to live "at a pace established by Edison, Marconi, and Ford," to use his words. Living in the country, however, has its two sides, as does living in the city. No one has communicated this better than Aesop with his fable, "Town Mouse and Country Mouse," a story Emily had recently read aloud to me. I saw weeds, bug bites, months of preserving, being snowed in and worrying if the wood would hold out, all the while trying to think up a different dish with potatoes or flour while waiting for the garden to produce something green in springtime.

The thick clouds were barring the sunshine from us but the fog had thinned. In town Michael slowed his pace as we reached the streets that had once been our neighborhood.

He asked, "Do you miss it?"

"Only a little," I answered.

Michael found a parking spot on Main Street, our old stomping ground. "Here it is," he said, "Tony has the best shoes in town." Michael was remarkably happy with money in his pocket. He held his bright expression as we stepped up to the shop and he opened the door. But as the bell tinkled and the door closed behind us, I felt flushed. Tony would have to take off my shabby old shoes in order for me to try on a new pair. I had to swallow my pride in one gulp. Michael was looking at the men's shoes to give me room to peruse. Perhaps he sensed my embarrassment. I sat down with three styles of shoes in my hand and Tony, the Italian shopkeeper, slipped off my old shoes.

"Stand here, please," he ordered as he checked the length and width of my feet in his metal measurer. He nodded and then disappeared behind a red curtain. I waited. To add to my awkward feelings, the door opened, tinkling the bell, and a pretty young lady sauntered across the shop to the display of the latest styles in high heels. We cordially exchanged smiles with her. Then she glanced down at my stocking feet but made her eyes dart elsewhere. How silly I was being about buying a pair of new shoes!

"Hello, Tony," Michael said, when the shopkeeper appeared with his boxes and knelt down before me. "I shall wither away," I thought, but just then Michael sat down beside me and put his arm around me.

"Your lady has good taste in shoes," Tony said to Michael. To the young lady Tony said, "I'll be with you in a minute or two, Miss Pinkette."

"No need. You know I like looking," she said. I noticed how well her dress fit and how its colors accentuated her strawberry-blonde hair. Apparently young ladies were wearing their hair fuller and longer and skirt lengths had shortened to new heights—just below the knee. I noticed, too, that her nail polish was the exact shade of her lipstick. Nail polish wouldn't last two hours on my hands.

All attention was now on me walking to and fro—in new shoes. "A little loose in the heel," I told Tony, and that pair was switched for another. Meanwhile I became aware of a smidgen of my own vanity as it occurred to me how I disliked the in-between months of pregnancy—when a woman's waistline is non-existent, but it isn't yet obvious by her figure that she is expecting. I walked to and fro some more, making my appraisal. "These fit splendidly," I announced.

"Take your time, sweetheart. Are you sure?" Michael asked. I walked back and forth one more time to humor him.

"Do you like these? I do," I said, happy that they fit. I find few material things in life more satisfying than a pair of new shoes.

"We'll take shoe polish to match, please," Michael told Tony.

"Certainly," Tony said. "Would you like me to wrap up these for you?" He held up my old shoes. They were a pitiful sight when displayed like that.

"No, wrap the new ones, please? It's too wet a day to wear them."

"Of course." He took the new pair off my feet and wrapped them in tissue paper. Then he slipped my well-worn shoes onto my feet in so elegant a manner it was as if they were Cinderella's glass slippers. "Looks like you gotta good use outta these. My mama, she did the same. She was on her feet a lot. I got seven brothers and sisters. She worked ha-a-rd. 'Papa,' she'd say, 'no break in my new shoes ayet,' she'd tell him. She went to confession every day but only wore her new shoes for baptisms, birthdays, first communions, weddings, and funerals."

Standing outside the shop, I said to Michael, "I like that Tony."

"I always have, too," he said. "Which way should we walk?"

"That way," I pointed.

Before we took a step, who did we see marching down Main Street but Mr. Fortesque, of all people? "Look. It's Mr. Fortesque!" Michael exclaimed. Mr. Fortesque had his face set to the pavement, intent on reaching his destination in good time. He was approaching us but was unaware we were there.

Michael woke him up to the fact. "Mr. Fortesque!" he called.

"Michael, my good man. What a surprise to see you – and your good lady." He raised his hat in greeting. "Out for the day together? Jolly good." His rust-colored hair was disheveled. He was wearing a long black trench coat and had an umbrella hooked over his arm. Without waiting for our reply he told us he was meeting someone, would be late for an appointment if he tarried, and stepped into the shoe shop.

"He hates not to be punctual," Michael told me.

"I'm sure," I confirmed.

We decided to walk to the park first. The shoebox was stowed away in the car and, with our picnic basket in hand, we took in some leisurely window shopping as we made our way to the old covered bridge that crossed a pool of calm water. Bridgeton is so named because of its many little bridges that cross and re-cross over its ubiquitous stream. We settled on a bench, one of the wrought iron and wood benches that had been strategically placed when the town was reviving its image. I first opened a Thermos of sweet milky tea, made just the way Michael liked it. Then I unwrapped our sandwiches. I couldn't remember when last we had shared a quiet lunch together, all to ourselves. I nibbled happily, shook the crumbs off my napkin, and fed my crusts to the ducks.

"You always spoil the birds," Michael remarked.

"I spoil you, too, darling," I responded.

"You're right, there," he agreed.

"I ought to be feeding my cardinals," I said. It felt peaceful to be watching the slow-moving water in the deserted park. One would never guess that Main Street's pavement full of cars was just two blocks away. Nothing about the water sparkled as it would have if the sun had been shining, but we were content.

"I like these cookies," Michael said.

"Emma made them," I said. "Which reminds me, she needs more shredded coconut. It's expensive, I know, but since she's keeping an eye on the children and Blackberry Inn today..."

"We'll get the coconut," he said.

"The shop is a bit out of the way, somewhere on Chestnut Street," I said. "They have the canned salmon I like, too, for my croquettes."

"I know a shortcut through that alley behind that row of shops," he pointed.

The sky started to mist, so I began placing our picnic things back into the basket. Michael watched me. "Your hands are so dainty. Did I ever tell you how beautiful they are? Always serving, loving, making something. One of the first things I noticed about you when I first met you were your hands." I felt my second flush of the day. I was not a blushing bride. I had been married to this man for years.

"Your kind and handsome voice was what first attracted me," I said. He seemed pleased at this, since I rarely verbalized these kinds of things.

"Really?" he asked, cupping my hands in his, as though he were holding a little sleeping bird.

"Sincerely," I said. The sky got darker. The mist turned to drizzle so I quickly finished filling the basket. Michael opened our one umbrella and we headed off down the alley, walking arm in arm, trying to keep dry, but getting soaked by the drizzle nonetheless.

The alley was quiet. No children were playing. No wash hung on the lines. Its eerie atmosphere made the overcast day seem grayer. "I'm not used to walking down deserted alleys in the rain," I said.

"No, of course not," he sympathized. Then Michael exclaimed, "Look up there! I think I see Mr. F. again! Isn't that he?"

"Where?"

"He's walking up those steps to the second floor."

"It *is* Mr. Fortesque," I said, because as we got closer, I was certain. Michael brought the umbrella down closer to our heads, reacting involuntarily, and we took slower steps. We watched Mr. Fortesque as he waited at the top of the stairs at the door of an apartment. He turned his head and, with it, his umbrella, nervously right and left.

"Did you see that?" I said in almost a whisper. "He looks positively furtive." When the door was opened only halfway, Mr. Fortesque took a quick step inside sideways.

"I don't think he saw us," Michael said.

"No," I said. It felt like we were spying on him. When we came to the stairs we looked up, but could spot no number or markings on the door whatsoever that would distinguish it from the others in the row.

"That's strange," said Michael, and we kept walking.

"That *is* strange," I said. But we said no more.

Across town we stepped through the door of the booksellers' drenched with rain. I told the man about our book order and he slipped into a back room to find it. Meanwhile Michael and I browsed. My wet hair, minus all curl, was hanging in my face by this time, so I tucked it up into my hat. After spending time in the biography section, I selected two that looked irresistible, adding them to a copy of *Winnie the Pooh* by A. A. Milne, *The Railway Children* by Edith Nesbit, and *A Little Princess* by Frances H. Burnett, that I already had in my hand. Of the biographies, one was the life of Puritan John Eliot, missionary to the Indians of New England. The other was the story of William Penn.

"Hi," Michael said. "So much for thrift. I see we're both guilty."

"Can we afford this?" I asked, clutching my stack.

"I think so," he said. "It will flatten my wallet though."

I raised my eyebrows. "That's what I mean."

"Don't worry. I have two dollars saved under the mattress," he said reassuringly.

"Good thinking," I said. "Let's see your books."

He showed me *Wind in the Willows* by Kenneth Grahame and *The Story of Doctor Doolittle* by Hugh Lofting, and together we laughed out loud for the first time all day.

"You're just as extravagant," I said, but mixing practicality with impulse, I added, "Let's keep a couple of books for each child hidden for Christmas."

"Okay," he said.

I waited in the shop until Michael brought the car around. We drove back to Appleton hungry, tired, and wet, but with souls renewed.

"It feels good to be going home," Michael said.

"East West, Home is Best," I said. And thought to myself, "I guess that's what Blackberry Inn should be called."

Chapter Seven

The Church Needs Cleaning

Kindness is in our power, even when fondness is not.

Samuel Johnson

earing the men sing on Sunday morning was a treat. It helped me focus on the attributes of our heavenly Father. "Immortal, Invisible, God only wise" is an old Welsh melody that recalled the days of Michael's youth. After the sermon I said to him, "So that's what you've been humming around the house. You didn't tell me you were singing this morning."

"I thought you liked surprises," he said.

"I liked it very much," I told him.

Emma was happy to see the Miss Goslins back in church. I wore my new shoes for the first time. Dora noticed.

Penelope and I had a brief chat. She said that she and Pastor were going to be in Bridgeton on the coming Saturday and asked a little hesitantly if I could take over her chore of dusting and sweeping the church and straightening the hymnbooks. I told her I could. "Seth and Sarah will help," she said. "Benjamin will be home tackling the woodpile. We're behind in getting up our wood because of the bountiful harvest."

"We are, too," I said. "Donald and Emily will be happy to help, especially if it means playing with your children."

"Thank you, Carol. You're a dear," Penelope said, much relieved. She disliked the job of asking people to do things for the church.

It was another week of lessons and we were now in the thick of it. Rather than be distracted by the telephone installers, I let Donald observe, ask his questions, and then get back to his work. I settled the children into their new arithmetic books. Upon closer inspection, the work in Donald's book appeared to be more challenging than I had expected. I reminded myself that arithmetic is accomplished by increments and that the motto of "inch by inch, it's a cinch" applies. And if Donald got stuck on anything, Michael would be able to help. Donald, however, dove into the work undaunted. He liked the challenge of a new level of work. Emily liked the colored pictures and wrote out her problems dutifully.

I was pleased with *The Wonderland of Science.* Its well-written chapters helped a child to understand the material world he lived in, which Miss Mason believed to be of principal importance. The first chapter was on different kinds of plants. After reading the chapter, we spotted some mushrooms. It prompted us to keep our eyes open for fairy rings and we were very happy to find one in the orchard. We left some damp bread out to get moldy, and made a "sponge"— watching yeast foam in a bowl of sugar water and flour. This chapter also included a few pages on bacteria, with drawings of both helpful and harmful germs. It helped to answer Donald's question on the need for sterilization.

With my mind on germs, I took advantage of the sun one afternoon, scrubbing the wooden draining board above and below. After it had thoroughly dried in the sun, I gave Donald the chore of rubbing it with oil. While he was at it, I also gave him the wooden spoons, cutting boards, and our two large wooden salad bowls to oil.

In the meantime Emily and I cut out some baking powder biscuits for supper. She likes to use her hands. Supper was my daily chore. Every morning Emma made breakfast for the household and set her wheat bread to rise. But most days she and I worked in the kitchen together, especially when there were guests.

<hr>

That weekend there were no guests—not even Mr. Fortesque, for he was away. Saturday morning Michael and I were sitting on the kitchen stoop together after an early breakfast. The cool air was refreshing and brisk. The fragrance of cut hay drifted our way, reviving our senses. Draining his cup of its last sip of coffee, Michael placed it on the saucer and said, "You're looking at that woodpile, aren't you?"

I admitted that I was. A mountain of work was waiting for him. Wintertime, however, waits for no man.

"Bob hasn't split any of *his* yet," Michael said calmly.

I was puzzled. "He hasn't?" I frowned. "He and Dad always would have made a good start of it by now. Anyway, I thought you were enamored with country life," I said rather too smartly.

"I'm enamored with you," he said. This brought a smile to my face, as Michael hoped it would.

<hr>

We discussed the day awaiting us. "I'm off to Bob's with Donald, but I'll drop you at the church on the way."

"You've been a big help to Bob."

"He's been a big help to us with milk and eggs. Have you seen their garden this year? It's enormous. He's been driving into Bridgeton once a week, sometimes twice, with his truck full of surplus vegetables. Somehow he's made good connections."

"Hmm, I hope he doesn't overwork himself," I said.

"Exactly," Michael said in a sympathetic tone.

"I was planning to have Donald as my floor sweeper today at the church," I said.

"That's fine," Michael said. "He can walk over to Bob's when he has finished there. He's surrounded by ladies all week. It's good for him to be with fellows on the weekend."

⌒⌒

September is the time of year to be planting or separating bulbs. As Donald, Emily, and I approached the front lawn of the church, I recalled how densely packed its daffodils were last spring. A little separating now would bring a better display of flowers next year, but it would entail more than a couple of hours of hard digging, and so I gave up on the idea because of my condition.

"Mom, should Emily and I go next door to get Seth and Sarah?" asked Donald.

"Yes," I said, and off they ran.

⌒⌒

Opening the front door of the church, an offensive odor resembling sour milk and billy-goat assailed my nose. Country folk often come to church unaware of what they bring on the soles of their shoes, and I knew the building needed more than sweeping and dusting today. It could use a good mopping. I opened two small windows and left the front doors ajar. When the children arrived, Emily said, "Mommy, what smells bad?"

"I'm not sure," I said. I handed out brooms to the boys and dusters to the girls. "Give special attention under the pews where dried mud accumulates," I told the boys, "and sweep well into the corners, too, please." The girls dusted the pews and I straightened the hymnals. The sanctuary is small, so it wasn't long before the girls reached the pulpit.

"Mommy, come quick, there's a man on the floor!" Emily called to me. Sarah gasped.

"What?" I said. The boys and I hurried to the front of the church. Looking down at a man in rags, I told the children, "He's a hobo."

"A hobo?" Donald questioned.

"It stands for homeward bound," I simply said. The man was asleep on his stomach, his head turned to one side. He stirred a little from the noise of our talking. His brown suit of clothes was malodorous and threadworn, and had been mended all over by an inexperienced hand, probably his own. His brown hair was matted, and his skin was creased with dirt and exhaustion and tanned a somber color, like earth itself. The hands of this man of small stature were large enough

to be those of a blacksmith, which told me that they had long been acquainted with manual labor.

"Mrs. Weaver, what should we do? Should I run over and get Benjamin?" Seth asked. I tried to think quickly. The man rolled over onto his back and opened his eyes.

"Elspeth," he said, staring at the ceiling, then he closed his eyes again. It was a weak, pathetic plea.

I hurried the children along, worried that they might hear a string of interesting expletives from the stranger.

"Donald, run to Uncle Bob's and tell Dad that we found a hobo in the church and to bring Uncle Bob's truck right away."

"Yes, Mom." Donald dropped his broom and ran.

"Seth, you get Benjamin and tell him that we need a jug of warm, not cold, milk."

"Yes, ma'am."

"Girls, you go to Sarah's and wait for me there."

Alone in the quiet church, I seated myself on the front pew near the man and found that I was trembling. Staring up at the colors of the stained-glass window before me, I prayed. Then the hobo opened his eyes again. They were big hazel eyes—as soft as a fawn's—and edged by long dark lashes that gave away his age. He was a young man. He looked in my direction without meeting my eyes and spoke again, "Elspeth?" His lips were dry and cracked, like those of a man who had crossed a desert. When he tried to sit up, he collapsed to the floor. It was then that I felt more pity for him than fear. I recalled some lines of poetry, although I could not recall whose lines they were. They were reminiscent of my school days, lines I had once had to memorize:

> *I am oppressed*
> *I wander like the desert wind*
> *With no place to rest*
> *Blowing like the dust.*

Thank goodness Seth and Benjamin returned then with the milk. I knelt down and held the jug near to the stranger's face and he lifted his head. Grasping the jug with a shaky hand, he drank in thirsty, noisy gulps, much of the milk running down either side of his chin. When he had drained the jug, he collapsed again, as if lifting his head was too much effort.

I whispered to the boys, "He's very weak. We'll let him rest. Mr. Weaver will know what to do with him when he gets here."

By Benjamin's open countenance and lucid blue eyes I could tell that he was a thinking lad. Close up I could see his nose was as freckled as the belly of a trout. "He must've gotten off the train at the Forest Green station," he said thoughtfully, "and made his way here. But it's a long way to walk. And who is he?"

"That's what we'd all like to know," I said. "I suppose we shouldn't be staring at him. Let's let him be until the men get here." Restless, I returned the brooms and dusters to their closet and found a mop with which to clean up the milk. Upon hearing Bob's truck pull up, I let go a long sigh and stopped trembling.

In Blackberry Inn's kitchen Emily excitedly shared with Grandma about our finding the hobo. I made the two girls a sandwich and they went outside to play.

When Emma set the kettle to boil, I knew a chat was forthcoming, so I sat at the table. Naturally she wanted to hear my side of the story, too. "We get so few hobos in Appleton because we are far from any railroad tracks," Emma said. "Can you describe him?"

I did, and when I told her that he had called out the name, Elspeth, she raised a knowing eyebrow. "Several years ago," she said, "a young Scotch-Irish couple moved into Woodrow McDuff's old place. Woodrow hired the husband to work in his apple orchard and do other needed work on his farm. The couple kept to themselves entirely. Her name is Elspeth, a form of Elizabeth I believe. Her husband, your hobo, is Darby O'Reilly. Elspeth's mother lived with them. About a year or so after, a baby was born, Mr. McDuff left the farm, and Mr. O'Reilly went away to find other work. One day none of them were ever seen again."

"Is that all you know?" I asked.

"Only that the people of the church brought baskets of food, but the O'Reillys would accept no charity."

I imagined that one of "the people" was Emma. "Sounds sad," I sighed. "Well, I had better get supper started."

"Sit for awhile and drink your tea; then we'll fix supper together," she coaxed. She was wise enough to know that the day had unfolded only half its drama.

Chapter Three

We Were Once Strangers

*My hope is built
on nothing less
Than Jesus' blood
and righteousness.*
Edward Mote

ow are you?" I asked Michael when he trudged up the porch steps to the kitchen. "You're soaking wet. I'd better run you a bath or you'll catch cold."

"That sounds wonderful, sweetheart. I think I used every muscle today," he said, rubbing his left shoulder. "Bob's driving Sarah home," he added.

"Where's the hobo?" I had to ask.

"He's here, resting in the carriage house."

"Here? I didn't think you'd bring him here." My emotions were stirred.

"We're the ones who found him. I talked with Emma outside. She said he could stay. It *is* Emma's...um. Shouldn't she have a say?" posed Michael.

"But he can't come inside." I said, in more of plea than a command.

"Why not?" Michael said.

"Well, for one thing," I lowered my voice, "you never know what might hop, creep, or crawl out of his hair."

Michael laughed. "We *cut* his hair and dunked him in the pond. He's been well fed, thoroughly scrubbed, lathered and shaved, *and* given a whole new set of clothes—some old trousers of Bob's—and a flannel shirt. Dora worked fast at shortening the hems of both, I might add." He ended his speech with, "What a day."

My conscience was nudged. Humility put me in my place. "I see. Come on, darling, it's your turn for a bath," I said. Together we walked up the stairs while I fed his ear with what Emma had told me about the O'Reillys.

At the conclusion of this Michael said, "I'm glad we've found *something* out. He was so listless that we couldn't get anything out of him except, 'She's gone.'"

I was glad Blackberry Inn had no guests. Oh, but we did have *one*. He was in the carriage house.

That evening after Mr. O'Reilly was asleep and we were seated at the dining room table just starting our dessert, Donald stated the obvious, "The telephone." It was our first time to hear it ringing. Emma popped up and hastened to the sitting room to answer it.

"Well, we know the ringer works," Michael said. I could hear the faint tones of Emma's voice far off. She talked for some time.

When she came back to her seat at the table, she looked at Michael and said, "It's for you. It's Mr. Fortesque."

After their Saturday baths I read to the children in their bedroom. Emily said, "Mom, the hobo is poor, isn't he?"

"Of course he's poor," Donald interrupted. He knew immediately by the look I gave him that his unthinking comment had been a rude one. "Sorry," he said.

"Are we rich?" Emily was following a train of thought.

"In a way we are. Daddy has work and the hobo hasn't any work, not yet. His name is Mr. O'Reilly."

"Should I pray that Mr. O'Reilly gets work?" Emily asked.

"Yes, darling," I said, "that's a good thing to pray for."

Sunday morning, after the children and I had finished dressing, we entered the kitchen. Michael and Mr. O'Reilly were sitting at the table together eating the eggs, muffins, and coffee that Emma had served. Apparently, Mr. O'Reilly had finally revived.

"I am very grateful for what you've all done for me," he said.

Michael introduced us. "Pleased to meet you," he said, as if he had never seen me before, "and call me Darby."

Michael said, "Darby is coming to church with us this morning."

"Oh, how nice," is all I said. Emma was beaming while she placed another muffin on Darby's plate and poured him more coffee.

In the car Emily sat in front so that Darby could fit in back. He was quiet. Upon entering the church, various members of the congregation greeted him with interest. But when we walked up the aisle to take our seats, Darby lagged behind and would go no further than the back pew. Directly after the sermon he vanished.

Emma said, "I know where Darby used to live."

"Please show me," said Michael.

Our car climbed up a narrow road to an abandoned farmhouse. The house seemed solid enough but the ramshackle columns of the crooked front porch made the building appear to be resting dolefully on a pair of crutches. Michael parked in the shade and walked up to the house to look around. He returned, walking slowly with a man in despair, whose eyes were still red from weeping. Once Darby got in the car he said plainly, "The house is filled with bats. They must've come in through the chimney." I shuddered at the thought.

～～

Later that day Michael, Emma, and I listened to Darby's story of misadventure. After Woodrow McDuff moved away without explanation and without payment to Darby, Darby became a man-of-the-road, an itinerant laborer, which carried him farther and farther away from home. He mailed money to his wife regularly, and in this way Elspeth was able to take care of their baby, Andrew, and her mother for six months. Eventually she had money to spare, and in every letter she urged Darby to come home. He would always tell her, "One more month," because he liked being able to send money. Then he was tempted by greed. A group of men convincingly explained their plan of action to him and asked him to join them in dropping cargo out of a moving train to later sell. Supposedly its rich owner wouldn't miss it. But he did miss it, justice was served, and Darby ended up in prison. He wrote his wife and told her all, asking for her forgiveness. She never wrote back.

"I did a bad thing, but I'm sorry for what I did, very sorry," Darby told us. "It's been so long since I've seen me wife and son. I've *got* to try to find them." Without another word he fled through the kitchen door, stumbled down the porch steps, and hid himself in the carriage house, leaving us speechless. I could tell, however, that wheels were turning in Michael's mind.

～～

My brother Bob stopped by with Dora and the baby that Sunday afternoon. The weather was fair and the air cool. Michael explained to Bob the reason for Darby's heartache. Together the men went into the carriage house to encourage Darby and convince him to stay at Blackberry Inn and rest until he was stronger. They suggested that meanwhile he ought to make his house ready.

Dora balanced Jonathan on her hip while she and I and Emily took a Sunday stroll. We walked around the cemetery. "Ooh, look pokeberries. They're plump and ripe and will make just the pink I need," Dora said. "Would you carry a bunch for me?" She began breaking off the stems with one hand. "I've collected goldenrod for yellow and sassafras root bark for brown. Whenever I go for walks, I keep my eyes open for plant dyes."

"Does this mean you were able to tackle that bag of wool?" I asked. Over the summer I had become aware of a burlap bag in the corner of the barn.

"Oh, yes!" she answered victoriously. "I enjoy the spinning, but it was a job getting it picked, washed, and carded first, I can assure you. I'm happy to say I have yarn ready for dying."

"Getting the right pink is important," I affirmed. I was glad I was still wearing my apron, since the pokeberries she handed me were known for their staining power. "Emily, pokeberries might look good to eat, but they're poisonous. Keep them away from your mouth." Emily had been listening to her aunt and me talk and was squishing the juicy berries between her fingers at the same time.

"It *is* a pretty pink," she said.

Dora's ability to spin was learned entirely out of a book. She had a late model spinning wheel, not an antique, and kept one sheep that Bob sheared for her as best he could. I prefer to purchase my yarn but I admire Dora's resourcefulness. "One of those big antique wheels would be just the thing to decorate the corner of Emma's wide hearth," I said, while waving my arm in a big circle as if tracing its size. "It would lend the sitting room authenticity."

"Oh, those are walking wheels. The wheel is turned with a hand while walking back and forth. A colonial housewife would walk *miles* with that wheel. I'd rather sit while I spin."

As one knitter to another, I asked, "Do you have a sweater planned?"

"Yes, one with a pale yellow background and a Fair Isle border pattern of pink roses and green leaves."

"I can't wait to see it when it's done. We women are always dreaming and planning ahead, aren't we?" I mused, and we walked in the direction of the house, the cool breeze in our faces. We could see my brother and Michael leaving the carriage house without Darby.

Donald ran up to us with something in his hand. "Look Mom, Butterscotch laid her first egg!" he said, holding it up for all to see.

"It's a large one," I said.

"May I hold it?" asked Emily.

"I found it, Em," was Donald's reason for being its keeper.

"Please?" Emily tried again.

"Just for a second," was as far as Donald's generosity would take him on this momentous occasion.

On Dora's hip little Jonathan was the perfect height for reaching for the egg in Emily's hand, but Donald instantly asked for his egg back. With it firmly in his grasp, he and Emily made a beeline for the house. They were going to find Emma to share their excitement with her, I was certain. "Good for the bairns," I thought.

Dora and I met up with the menfolk in the kitchen where Emma was stirring a pot of hot chocolate for us. It filled the room with an inviting fragrance.

Bob told Emma, "He's agreeable for now. He said he would stay."

"Oh, good, good," Emma said.

To me, Bob said, "It seems, Carol, that Darby is a seeker of God as well as his wife and son. That's why you found him in the church."

"Oh, good," Emma said again. "This is so good." She let go of the stirring spoon, clapped her hands together once or twice, and said, "Well done, Bob and Michael." She was the picture of joyous spontaneity. She gave them each a brief hug for sharing the Lord, as if they were her own sons.

With the dairy cows waiting, Bob and Dora left promptly after finishing their mugs of hot chocolate. That evening Michael said, "I have an idea." He dialed the telephone and spoke with Mr. Fortesque. But I didn't hear about it until later. Michael gathered us together in the sitting room. He sat next to Donald and opened his Bible. Emma sat on the other side of Donald with her crocheting. From where I sat with Emily I could see the entrance to the kitchen.

"Here in Matthew five," Michael said, "Jesus is giving a long teaching for His disciples, the longest in the Bible. In a kind of poem He tells us the way our attitudes are supposed to be. Donald, read verses one through three."

I thought I saw a shadow move in the kitchen. It could have been the curtain blowing or it might have been Darby. The sun was setting on the other side of the house and the kitchen was full of shadows.

"*...Blessed are the poor in spirit,*
For theirs is the kingdom of heaven," Donald finished.

Michael then gave his commentary, which was relevant and beautifully spoken. "We come to God with our spiritual pockets empty. We can all say, 'In myself there dwells no good thing apart from you,

God.' To be poor in spirit is to be sorrowful over my sin. 'On this one will I look: On him who is poor and of a contrite spirit' (Isaiah 66:2). A man isn't blessed when he's at the end of his rope. He is blessed when he *knows* he's at the end of his rope. Humility is recognizing that we are needy. God's people know they don't do as well as they set out to do. Without Christ we are *all* destitute hobos with nothing in our spiritual pockets. As the hymn says, 'Nothing in my hand I bring, simply to Thy cross I cling.'"

Emma nodded her head amidst her steady crocheting, as an amen to this part of Michael's message. Behind her I could just make out Darby's hand on the back of a chair in the darkening shadows.

"But the poor in spirit can be happy because Jesus came and saved them. We are happy people because we are forgiven. We who were once strangers to God were made to be children of God. He is making a home for us in heaven and wants us to live for Him here on earth."

I heard a sneeze coming from the kitchen. So did all of us. It made us all look up. Then the kitchen door quietly clicked closed. I prayed Darby would be convicted by Michael's message of hope, because it would lead him to the right place: the foot of the cross.

Chapter Nine

Rabbit Pie

Work of any description adds to one's happiness.
Grandma Moses

The window across from my bed revealed a sky as soft and gray as the breast of a mourning dove. I heard the noise of the rhythmic sawing of wood coming from the back of the house and assumed that Michael had gotten up extraordinarily early. The morning air can be bracing, and as a man who likes mornings, he would find these early hours best suited for such work. I stood at the top of the stairs, about to descend, but turned first to call out, "Children, I expect you down for breakfast very soon." When I entered the kitchen, Michael, to my amazement, was sipping a cup of coffee, comfortably seated across the table from Emma.

"I thought I heard sawing, I thought you..." I stammered.

"Darby's been at it for some time," Michael said, grinning boldly. "He says he won't keep eating our food without working. I agree with his ethics, don't you?" The night before, Michael had told me that all the positions were filled at the canning factory, but that he had expressed to Mr. Fortesque the need for a rat catcher. The rodents were a nuisance, and even though the floor was mopped each afternoon, sanitation would not be complete without the elimination of them. Therefore Mr. Fortesque had given his sanction for Michael to hire Darby for the task. This would mean only a very small source of cash, but it was a start. Michael stood up from the table, kissed me goodbye, and stepped outside calling, "Time to go, Darby."

All morning the gray sky let fall its gentle rain, which meant that Geraldine had to hang much of the wash in the cellar to dry. The children and I were cozy in the library with our lessons while the occasional breeze splashed raindrops on the windows, forming little rivulets on the glass. I displayed the second picture by Millet—another set of peasants. Chesterton claims that Millet's paintings "owe their strong appeal to no excellence of technique or coloring, but solely to the powerful human interest which they excite."

Without me having revealed the title of the painting, Emily asked, "They're not hobos, right, Mom? Because they're going to work."

"Yes, in the fields of France," I said. The peasants wore wooden clogs. The man held a wooden pitchfork over his shoulder, while the woman carried a large basket upside down over her head, its handle under her chin. Emily surmised that they were walking to, not from, work. Otherwise wouldn't her basket be full of potatoes or something?

Donald read aloud a good part of our poem, "Hiawatha's Fasting." I had read it with proper cadence the week before and he was doing a fine job of imitating what I had shown him. But when it came to making a drawing of an American Indian for his history notebook, he was disgusted. "I can't draw faces," he moaned.

"Never mind," I said. "You can draw the things that make up Indian life." Donald was okay with that. He drew a wigwam and Emily drew a papoose that resembled a baby doll.

I was happy that I was already hearing a more steady flow of narration from Emily, proving that she had a good understanding of what we read. I contented myself with the fact that this was, indeed, as Miss Mason claimed, the best way for a student to acquire knowledge from books. But Emily was painstakingly slow at copy work. I had to be watchful of how much time she spent on it. Yet her work was done neatly and I knew that as the weeks progressed, so would her proficiency.

Miss Mason had warned never to let a child dawdle over lessons, or to sit dreaming with his book before him. A mother's tact and vigilance is needed, she said, to guard against the child forming what she called "the habit of inattention." I remembered reading that, when a child grows lackadaisical over a lesson, it is time to put it away. "Let him do another lesson," she wrote, "as unlike the last as possible, and then go back with freshened wits to his unfinished task."

I had made it a point the year before to prevent Emily from dawdling by keeping her lessons short and making certain they were bright and pleasant. Her new habit of attention and her ability to narrate were just two of the things that had brought my Emily back to life. When she had attended school in Bridgeton, her light had grown dim and she had started to fall through the cracks of learning. In only a few months of home teaching with Miss Mason's tried and true method, I was watching my daughter blossom. This year she was blossoming even more.

In school, Donald, too, had nearly lost his sense of wonder. Our previous year's outdoor nature observations, and Miss Mason's advocacy of keeping a nature notebook, had helped to bring back his sense of wonder. He also no longer found reading a drudgery after I replaced his readers with books by individual authors. For these reasons I wanted to keep teaching my children at home rather than send them off to the village school.

I handed Donald the biography of John Eliot for his silent reading, telling both children a little about Eliot's work of learning the language of the New England Indians so that he could communicate the gospel to them. Later, I told them, he worked long and hard to translate the Bible into their language and his labor of love resulted in many converts.

After their arithmetic pages were completed, I had Donald read aloud to us from "The Changing of the Seasons," the next chapter in our science book. The chapter was illustrated with a watercolor scene of what looked to be a perfect day in October: a blue cloudless sky, a horse grazing in front of a farm that was surrounded by shade trees all ablaze in orange and red leaves. He read about chlorophyll bodies beginning to disappear in deciduous trees when the temperature drops, about evergreen trees, and about hibernation. One example given of a hibernating animal was the bat with not one but two illustrations. I couldn't help thinking of Darby and the population of bats in his own house, and of the quantity of dirt they left behind.

I postponed spelling for last, perhaps because it was my least favorite subject to teach. Keeping to tradition, we kept our tiresome lists of words. I found, however, that dictating passages from *Black Beauty* made the subject of spelling more interesting for us. I found that I could also use these same passages to teach Donald grammar. After pointing out examples showing that the verb of a sentence is always part of the predicate, the aroma of Emma's bread baking in the oven lured us into the kitchen. Here the children had an informal French lesson with Geraldine, who had just finished hanging up her last basket of wash in the cellar. I tied on my apron with lunch in mind.

There was a knock on the kitchen door. When I opened it, I found myself face-to-face with Darby standing on the threshold. He presented me with a gift—two pairs of rabbits he had hunted. He was holding them up by their feet, and lifted them higher for my inspection. I stepped outside. The rain had stopped, the sky was still a light gray, and the smell of wood smoke hung in the air. All across Appleton home fires were burning.

"What's this?" I asked.

"These are for supper," Darby said happily. "Elspeth used to make rabbit pie. Do you know how to make it?"

"With these I could make four," I told him. "Thank you. What a nice surprise."

"I'll have them skinned for you straight away," he said. "Then I'll be off to start cleaning me house. Does anyone in the village tan skins?"

"Yes, Mr. Pease might tan, or know someone who does. He plays the organ at church, but you haven't met him yet, have you? He lives on Paw Print Road between here and the village. A signpost outside his barn says Ferrier. It has a picture of a running horse on it," I added, in case he couldn't read.

"T'anks," he said in colloquial Irish.

I stepped into Emma's garden with a pair of scissors to snip a bouquet of herbs with which to flavor the pies. Straightening up from

my snipping, my eye caught the color of Emma's dress in the distance. She was in the cemetery. How solitary she appeared! I tucked the scissors and bouquet in my apron pocket and impulsively walked out to greet her. The cemetery was moist and green and still. "Maybe she'd rather be alone," I thought, as I got closer. But Emma was fond of people and company, and with good cheer she welcomed me.

"Carol. Hello. Out for a walk? The air after a rain is so clean and refreshing, isn't it?"

"This is where Dora found her pokeberries. I'd like to see the yarn she'll dye from them."

"When I first came to Appleton, there was an old woman who used to dye her own wool. The people called her Amazing Granny Grace. Her gravestone is that way." She pointed in the same part of the cemetery where my parents were buried.

"I vaguely remember my mother speaking of her," I said.

Emma and I strolled through the cemetery side by side. I showed her the herbs in my pocket, and informed her of Darby's offering. Then she stopped in front of a group of very small, very plain, gravestones. They were on the edge of the cemetery, along a little hillside of sorts, hidden from view of the pebbled pathway. Three of the stones simply had "baby" chiseled in them in capital letters. One said, "twins." Another had "Theodore." The difference in his dates was two years.

"Yours?" I asked.

"Yes, dearest. All of these babies are mine. But I've done my weeping. I just wanted to share this place with you." She smiled and put her arm around me, and I felt a closer friendship to her than I ever had before. This was the first time she had called me "dearest." Without further meanderings, we walked to the house in comfortable strides and entered the kitchen just as two loaves of bread were ready to take out of the oven. "In haste but never in a hurry," that was Emma.

I was glad that today was the day our iceman delivered a block for the icebox, because my double crust pies would make two meals.

A new block of ice meant that I could depend on the extra pies keeping well chilled until they could be eaten another day. The majority
of my afternoon was spent tending to the simmering rabbit, cutting
vegetables, rolling pie dough, and keeping watch over the baking. I
didn't mind the extra work because I knew leftovers would come of
it, and because I was hoping to cheer up a man in despair with his
favorite dish. Emily expressed the desire to help, so I let her roll out
some dough, too. I found her a small pie pan so that, when filled, she
could think of it as her own pie. Afterwards we cut a few more circles
of fabric for our yo-yos, but this was short-lived, and she soon set up
her paper dolls in her familiar place on the living room rug.

"Hello, sweetheart," Michael said. "Something smells wonderful."
"You'll never guess what," I said. "When did you get home?"
"A little while ago."
When I moved to the sink I could see Darby washing at the pump.
A basin, a bar of soap, a washcloth, and a bench had been provided
for him. Two towels were draped over Michael's arm. "Just washing up
for supper, darling," he said, as if it were a trite everyday matter to rid
oneself of bat dirt before coming to the table.

Supper was served and it was quite satisfying to see Darby's face
when the savory meal was set before him. His appetite was large and
he made hums of delight while chewing. At first I was rather taken
aback by the fact that he was wearing the cream-colored Aran pullover that I had knitted Michael during our first year of marriage.
Because the pullover was too big, he had to keep the sleeves rolled up.
True, by now it was fuzzy and threadworn, especially at the elbows.
Michael wore it only on weekends, to rake leaves in autumn, carry the
children piggyback, or carve pumpkins on the front porch.

Darby cleared his plate by using a piece of bread to sop up the
last bit of brown gravy. He then conveyed his compliments to the
cook and kept talking. "Galway, on the west coast of Ireland, is where

I'm from," he told us. "Off the coast is a group of islands, the Aran Islands. Me mom made me dad Aran pullovers just like this one," he said, as he placed his two hands across his chest. "This is a fisherman's sweater," he told the children. "Me dad was a fisherman. The yarn has sheep lanolin in it. That sheep's wool was the only t'ing that would keep a fisherman warm when it got wet. Twisting it into cables makes the pullover thicker. Ya see this stitch going up the middle here? It's called 'beehive.' It stands for hard work. And this is a ladder. It connects man to God. What do t'ese look like to ya?"

Donald said, "Ropes?"

"'Tis right, Donald. All seagoing vessels have ropes. Me dad taught me nautical knots. If you get some rope I'll show ya some."

"Swell," Donald said, and he scrambled out of the room without asking to be excused.

Darby looked at me and said, "'Tis special to me, this pullover."

"I'm glad," I said.

I felt better knowing my handiwork was so appreciated. Apparently it held even more sentimental meaning for him than it did for me. Michael sighed a short sigh and held my hand under the table. It was his way of saying thank you.

Chapter Ten

Emma's Birthday

Friendship is the nearest thing we know to what religion is. God is love, and, to make religion akin to friendship is simply to give it the highest expression conceivable to man.

John Ruskin

"Mommy, look!" Donald and Emily called together. When I entered their bedroom, they were standing at the window. It's funny how children expect you to respond to their invocation of "Mommy!" any time, from any room of the house. We are their earthly guardian angels.

"What is it?"

"Look at all the robins in our front yard," Donald pointed out.

"Ooh. The yard is covered with them. 'Birds of a feather flock together.' These robins are flocking together along their migration south to warmer weather. They'll be gone all winter. We will have to wait until March to see them again," I told the children. Although the yard was abundant with robins we could hear none of their flute-like melodies. Perhaps they were saving energy for their long flight ahead.

In the middle of lessons the telephone rang. I answered it and spoke with Mr. Fortesque who said he would be arriving that afternoon. Then he told me that today was Emma's sixtieth birthday. "But don't tell her I said so." I felt a tinge of embarrassment upon hearing her age, because I had thought Emma to be older and hadn't considered the effects of weathering on the devoted gardener. When I shared with him my desire for an impromptu party, he thought it a wonderful idea and apologized for not telling me sooner.

I hung up the telephone, the children of course wanting to know who had called. I told them the news. "Let's make it a surprise."

"Are you going to make a birthday cake?" Emily asked.

"Yes. Would you like to make a card?"

"What should I say?"

"Grandma likes poetry. Why not copy a verse into her card?" I suggested. That took care of poetry reading and copy-work for the day. After the children's cards were decorated and hidden, we moved into the kitchen for arithmetic lessons so I could bake the cake. Emma could smell the cake baking, I knew, but we said not a word about it.

After lunch the children and I ventured out to take a long walk to Uncle Bob's to invite his family to our surprise dinner party. I was relieved to meet Dora in the village so that I didn't have to walk so far. "Looking forward to it," she said. "Are you getting ready for the Apple Butter Festival? I'm making apple tarts for the church fund—the ones where the pastry is folded over; you know, the ones that fit in the palm of your hand?"

"Oh, yes, no need for plates or forks. Wise choice," I said. "What's the fund for this year?" I asked.

"Penelope told me the walls of the church could use a new coat of paint."

"I agree with Penelope," I asserted.

Apples were on my mind. Although I had always canned apple-sauce and apple pie filling from the apples Bob brought me, the thought of him hard at work selling his surplus made me tell Dora, "We thought we'd scrounge in Emma's orchard to see what we could come up with for apples this year. It just might prove promising."

"Let me know how it turns out," she said.

＊ ＊

While the children of Appleton were still cooped up in the village school, my children and I were walking back home with four lemons, a pound of butter, and a bag of powdered sugar for the cake icing. The woods were sprinkled with asters, the last of the season's wildflowers. Bumblebees took from them their last sips of nectar. The tops of the maples looked like someone had recently set a match to them. They were on fire with color. In the weeks to come the bright orange flames would spread to the leaves below.

"Hey Mom, I just got hit by an acorn," said Donald.

"Hay is for horses," I corrected him, "not for mothers. It stands to reason that you might be hit by *something* in autumn. That's why the season is also called fall. Leaves, seeds, nuts, apples and acorns fall from the trees or bushes." More acorns pelted the road as a breeze caught the tops of the trees. I buttoned my trusty cardigan against the chill. As we walked, we crushed acorns under our feet, making a "snap, crackle" sound. Emily picked out the biggest, shiniest ones to put in her pockets.

With her eyes on the dirt road, she said, "Look, a woolly bear!" This, too, she picked up. The fuzzy caterpillar curled up in her hand. She carried it unafraid because we had observed the Isabella tiger moth in our Nature Study the year before and she was familiar with it. As we walked I shared some New England folklore with them. Our living in the country must have brought it to mind, for I had not thought of it when we lived in Bridgeton. It is believed that the severity of winter can be predicted by the amount of black on the caterpillar. "If you see more black than brown on the woolly bear," I told my children, "it will be a stormy winter. If the woolly bear is mostly brown, we can expect a mild winter."

With that said, we stopped in our tracks, because Donald expressed a desire to examine the caterpillar in Emily's hand.

"Black, Mom. The woolly bear has more black," he stated decidedly.

"Remember, it is only folklore," I said and we walked on.

~~~

I had one foot on the back stoop when my attention was turned toward the orchard. I tarried a moment to get a good look. Darby was rigging up sheets under the old trees. "What on earth is he doing?" I asked Emma when I entered the kitchen.

"He wants to reclaim the orchard. He even talked about pruning and grafting. He says he knows apples."

"Where'd he get the sheets?" was my next question.

"Not from the linen cupboard, Carol. They're my dustsheets from the attic. I've had things covered up there for years. Do you have a few minutes?" she asked. "I'd like you to look at some of them." The children ran out to the orchard to watch Darby while I followed Emma up the steep circular stairs.

"It's time to get back on your horse," she said, as we climbed. What she meant was that I hadn't been up the circular stairs since my nasty fall. I wasn't afraid of going up. It was coming down that I was uncomfortable with. Nevertheless, I bravely followed.

How different and more expansive the attic looked with so many things uncovered.

"Speaking of horses, what do you think of this one?" Emma asked, petting the mane of somebody's dream of a rocking horse. That somebody had built it out of wood, leather, and yarn. She combed her fingers through the mane to make it neat.

"Oh, it's a fabulous rocking horse," I said, admiring it.

"When Jonathan gets bigger he can ride it during his visits."

I didn't ask her if it had been made for Theodore. It looked like it had never been ridden. "Since I'm up here I may as well find my baby clothes and wash them," I said. After a minute or two of poking about, I found them. "Here they are."

"So this means you'll be telling the children?" In her day a lady rarely uttered a word to her offspring about an upcoming baby.

"Hmm, perhaps I *am* getting a little ahead of myself," I said to please her. I left my baby things where they were.

At that, Emma opened the lid of an old trunk. It creaked on its hinges, filling my nose with the musty smell of mothballs, and I sneezed. She announced, "I have some clothes that might fit Andrew."

"Andrew?

"Darby's lad. But Elspeth refuses charity. Perhaps I could make them a Christmas present," she added brightly. The clothes were carefully wrapped in tissue paper. The hunter green corduroy trousers she held up were darling. When she unwrapped the vest that matched, knit in a Donegal tweed, she pressed it to her bosom. The clothes in the trunk had probably been meant for Theodore. "Come to think of it, Andrew might like to give the rocking horse a try," she said, placing the vest carefully back in its nest.

I spoke my mind. "I hope Darby finds his wife, son, and mother-in-law. It must be dreadful for him."

"Yes, I'm sure it is," she agreed.

"Only a generous heart like yours, Emma, would wish to give away such special things. It isn't easy, is it?" I put myself in the position of the sympathizer for a change.

"Thank you, dear. I don't think I would've ever parted with them if you hadn't come here. It gives you pleasure, doesn't it, to see Darby wear the sweater you knitted for Michael? It would give me pleasure to see Andrew wear these clothes. I have a love for Darby's family now that I didn't have before. Dr. Cook was raised with *noblesse oblige,* and I acted accordingly, but I've stepped into the daylight about something lately." She paused and wore her contemplative face.

"Oh? What something is that?" I asked.

"Friendship," she answered. "I've learned that it's only by feeling our love that the poor will forgive us for our baskets of bread. I mean, I should have befriended Elspeth, even though I wasn't used to newcomers from so far away. I could have found another way to be friendly. Friendship is the key that opens locked doors. Friendship solves nearly every problem and soothes every ill. Isn't this the love Jesus spoke of?"

"Yes, I believe it is," I returned. We poked about some more in silence. And it was indeed quiet, for an attic that size muffled all

sounds from without. An attic is a sort of time capsule. It is its own peculiar time period existing oblivious to the rapidly changing world beyond. I untied a hatbox of my mother's that held a few childhood mementos. One was an alphabet sampler I had made at age eleven. It wasn't that I had remembered how old I was when I made it. My age happened to be recorded in tiny cross-stitches at the bottom of the sampler beside my name and under a motto that read, "Be Ye Always Kind and True."

"What's that, Carol—a sampler?"

"Yes, my girlhood sampler," I said holding it up for her to see.

"Those are barn owls, aren't they? And I like the tiny bleeding hearts."

"My father liked our hooting owls and my mother loved her bleeding heart flowers, so I worked them in," I said.

"It's sweet," she said.

Passing on to my little daughter the skills of needle arts was something I meant to do more of in the months and years to come. I rolled up the old linen sampler and left it for safekeeping where I had found it. I would save it as a surprise for the time when Emily was ready to make one.

I resisted any further rummaging because I sensed the kitchen calling me, and so I turned to go. "I like this old highchair," I pointed out along the way.

"It has certainly seen better days," Emma smiled, "and could do with some steadying."

With deliberate poise and caution I made my way back down the attic stairs, Emma leading the way. Donald found us at the foot of them. "Mommy, Grandma!" he said excitedly and a little out of breath from running. "I carried some apples back from the orchard. They're in the kitchen. You're right about apples falling, Mom. You should see what Mr. O'Reilly is making so the apples don't fall to the ground and get rotten."

I followed him downstairs to the kitchen. Emma—knowing full well what Darby was up to—followed, too. Donald handed me an apple. It was undersized, dimpled, and spotted. I bit into it. It was only a little sour. "Mmm, not bad," I said. Stepping out through the kitchen doorway with Donald, I looked out over the orchard again to acknowledge Darby's innovation. "We'll make good use of these apples. Thank you very much," I told my proud son. "And tell Mr. O'Reilly I said so, too." Suitably satisfied, Donald tore off toward the orchard. Emma and I shared a chuckle at his display of energy.

Enjoying a brief sit-down, I let Emily mix the icing. I showed her how to spread it on the cake in smooth swirls and tried not to show any concern for its lack of elegance. Later she and Donald dressed for the party in their Sunday best. I decided that my blue maternity dress was now a necessity and I welcomed its tucks and gathers in just the right places. Michael ran a bath for Darby. "I see he's graduated to indoor plumbing," I commented. Michael just laughed, startling me by putting his arm snuggly around my waist, and then pacified me further with a kiss. I surmised by these gestures that he had something more to tell me.

And he did. "Emma has cleared a place for Darby in the attic. The carriage house is too cold at night now."

"Yes," was my simple agreement.

Emma, aware of our party preparations, looked like she had stepped off the pages of an Edwardian fashion magazine. Her flowing dress in beiges and pinks, her long string of pearls, and her pearl-colored lace collar accented the soft tones of her hair. But the sight that boggled my mind was the appearance of Mr. Fortesque. He was wearing a new suit and, unlike his normal attire, there was not a wrinkle in it. The new suit made this stout man look almost slender and even somewhat taller. Apparently, the right tailor can do wonders.

Bob and Dora arrived and were dressed handsomely for dinner, too. Amidst my preparations, I asked Michael, "Now that we have some wood, would you light a fire in the dining room?" He obliged me without any jovial wisecracks, which at any other time would have been forthcoming.

Sensing the importance of the evening, Donald listened carefully to Emma's instructions, and brought down the old high chair from the attic for Jonathan. Darby set to work making one of the legs more secure. The red embroidered tablecloth, the best china, and a sparkling pitcher of lemonade made a festive table.

~~~

The flavors in the rabbit pie were particularly robust, the pies having marinated in the icebox. I balanced the savories with some sweeter side dishes, such as Emma's green tomato relish and my fried apples in brown sugar and cinnamon. The apples were those Donald had brought me.

While everyone was chatting about the upcoming Apple Butter Festival, I slipped away and lit the candles on the cake. As I reentered, Michael started the singing. It was a full chorus, a little overpowered by men's voices, moving Emma to one of her big grins.

"Very good," she said, and in one hearty whoosh, the candle flames turned to smoke. Darby was first to clap and the applause spread around the table. When it subsided, Emma looked over at Jonathan seated in the old high chair, and said, "Look at him. He's so cute. When did he learn to do that?" Jonathan was clapping his little hands, making no sound by it but entertaining himself nonetheless.

"It's his new thing, He started doing it this week," Dora told her.

~~~

I had just sat down after pouring another round of coffee when Emily came over and stood beside me to show me her newest paper creation. "Look at Colleen's dress," she said. It was evident to me that she had used the same colors that were in her grandmother's dress and must have gone off to make it just after she saw her in it.

Dora told her, "I like it."

Mr. Fortesque commented, too. "It looks like Grandma's dress," he said. I thought this uncommonly observant for a man. He added, "I'm wearing a new suit of clothes, too."

"Did you make it?" Emily asked.

"No, a beautiful lady picked it out for me," he said.

The room was suddenly silent. It was an awkward moment. We all knew that only men worked in a haberdashery and fitted men's clothes.

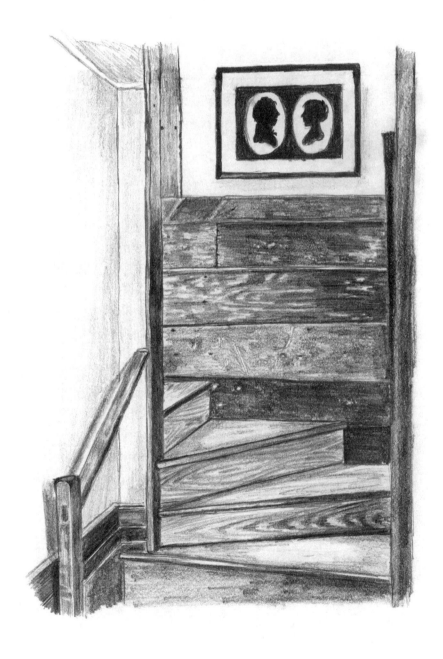

Bob broke the silence. He peeked at his pocket watch and caught Dora's eyes. "Cows," he announced laconically. They rose and bid Emma a good evening.

Emma beamed. "You've all made my birthday a very special one. Thank you."

"Bob, may I have a word outside?" Mr. Fortesque asked him, as Bob turned to leave.

My brother spoke his "Yup," and they departed. Dora made her polite good-byes, giving Emma a kiss on the cheek. The next thing we all heard was a loud cry bursting forth from the strong lungs of Jonathan as Dora, too, stepped outside to make her way to the truck.

"He was happy in the high chair," I said to Emma.

"Yes, he was," she replied inattentively. It was impossible to know whether she was gazing dreamily at the empty high chair or at the empty chair of Mr. Fortesque, because both were located at the same corner of the table.

Chapter Eleven

No Vacancy

*A friend is a
person with whom
I may be sincere.
Before him, I may
think aloud.*
Ralph Waldo Emerson

Emma once again answered the telephone. It rang frequently throughout the morning, interrupting Donald's history narration on Sir Francis Drake, and later our science lesson about the earth's axis and hemispheres. When Michael had mentioned advertising, I had assumed it would be for the spring, but apparently he had the Apple Butter Festival in mind. "Should I make Mr. Fortesque's room available if anyone else inquires?" Emma asked me. "For years he's had a room on weekends, but lately he has been coming earlier in the week instead." She seemed uneasy about this major change in her life.

"Let's ask him," I said.

At supper Mr. Fortesque had the smallest appetite of all. Afterwards he changed out of his suit and into corduroy trousers and a thick pullover. "I'm going out for a think in the garden," he informed us when he reentered the kitchen. "Join me later for a smoke?" he asked Michael. Michael nodded.

Because Emma hadn't brought up the subject, I took the initiative and jumped in with both feet. "Mr. Fortesque," I called, reopening the kitchen door, which had just closed behind him, "Mr. Fortesque!" I got his attention, and continued, "Blackberry Inn is filling up for the weekend. Will you be needing a room?"

"Aye, I'm looking forward to the Apple Butter Festival. Oh, I meant to ask you. Would you have a room for a lady as well?"

I froze. "A lady?"

"Aye."

"Hum, no. We only have one room left—the room we're reserving for you."

"Do you think Bob and Dora would put me up so she can have my room?"

"They'd probably be happy to," I said.

"Good. It's settled then. I'll run it by them tomorrow on my way home," he said. He bowed in a gentlemanly manner, touching the front of his tweed cap, then set off on his trudge, face to the ground, hands clasped behind him.

I was unequivocally unhinged. I grabbed the tea towel out of Michael's hand and tossed it aside. It landed in the soapy dishwater in the sink. "Michael, I can't do dishes now. I need to talk."

"Okay." He followed me into the far corner of the dining room. "What's this all about?" he said.

"I don't know where to start," I said in an energetic whisper. Yet, when I told him about reserving Mr. Fortesque's room for a lady friend, my sentence grew longer and longer. "...and his not showing up on weekends anymore, and his spiffy new suit, and his lack of appetite, and his thinks in the garden. And worst of all..." I hesitated, puffing out a large sigh.

"Worst of all what?" he asked calmly.

"Worst of all, his slipping into that back alley door. It's all so unseemly," I concluded. I had wound myself up in a tizzy.

"Carol, do you know what you're suggesting? Do you seriously imagine...?" He put a hand on my arm as if to steady me. "It's imponderable." He came closer, put an arm around me and stroked the back of my hair as though I were a child. And I felt like one. "Calm yourself," he said.

"Perhaps I *am* jumping to conclusions," I confessed, and then began to think more clearly. "Forgive me," I added, realizing that to shelter such suspicions, even for a passing moment, was to no longer hold Mr. Fortesque in high esteem.

Michael was both tactful and sensitive. "It's wrong to harbor a prejudice against him...however, I believe *something* is going on. It may be none of our business, but as we're his friends, we ought to be bearing one another's burdens." Then, turning it over in his mind some more, he added, "You *do* realize what this means, don't you?"

"No," I said.

"In confronting him I may soon be joining the ranks of the unemployed."

"Hmm," was all I added. And until we learned more, we made a resolution not to depreciate Mr. Fortesque.

That night I finished reading another chapter of *Black Beauty* to the children. After I closed the book, Donald and Emily started asking me questions about the Apple Butter Festival. "Mommy, Donald said there are going to be games and that I *have* to play them."

"It's going to be fun, Em. Seth said there's going to be the egg 'n spoon race, the three-legged race, and other games," Donald chimed in.

"Doesn't it sound like fun, Emily?" I encouraged.

All she said was, "Do I *have* to be in the games, Mommy?"

"No, you don't have to, but you might like the pony rides," I said. "Mr. Pease is always in charge of those."

Emily perked up. "There'll be ponies to ride like Merrylegs?" Merrylegs is the name of a pony in *Black Beauty*.

"Yes, but I don't think Mr. Pease's ponies will throw anybody off like Merrylegs decided to do. He lets his ponies take rests," I assured her.

The bedroom window was open a few inches, letting in the cool night air. But instead of closing it right away, I knelt down to the sill, and said, "Emily, listen." She knelt down beside me. "What do you hear?" I asked.

"Crickets," she said.

"Yes. Do they sound different, Donald?" I asked.

He answered, "It sounds like there aren't as many crickets chirping."

"Maybe, but there's something else. You can tell the night air is cooler because the crickets chirp more slowly. The cooler the air, the more time passes between their measured calls," I told them. The children found this fact interesting.

"If you listen, you can hear them with the window closed, but only faintly," I said. This helped my children settle for the night. Then in my bedroom I got into my nightgown and robe and sank into an easy chair with my mending basket in my lap. Some women find darning tedious. I find it soothing. Already Michael had holes in the socks I had knitted for him for his birthday. I sat in quiet relaxation with my needle. In a little while the man himself entered. His five o'clock shadow was gone. He gave me a clean-shaven kiss, which was a hint to me that he was feeling amorous, and sat down in his easy chair opposite me.

"I don't know how you manage to form holes in your socks so quickly," I said.

"It's one of my hidden talents," Michael smiled. "Those are my favorite pair. I wear them all the time. Why doesn't Geraldine mend them?" He took off his shoes, wiggled his toes to show me the socks he wore had no holes, then got up to put his shoes away, proud of himself for getting me to smile.

"We don't pay her to mend, only to wash and iron. Anyway, this is a task I don't mind doing. Did you have a good conversation with the men?"

"Darby's patience is wearing thin. He says the time has come to go out looking for his family." He was hanging up his tie behind the closet door.

"How's his house coming? Is it ready?" I asked.

"He works on it every afternoon he can, but no, it isn't...although the house doesn't matter to him as much as finding his family. Mr. F. is taking a sympathetic interest in the situation, by the way."

"Oh, really?"

"Yes. He persuaded Darby to leave the finding to him. He claims that he'd be far better at finding them than Darby because he knows so many people in the city. He's right, there. If Elspeth is living in Bridgeton or the neighboring towns, if anyone can find her, Mr. F. can. He has Darby's go-ahead and will begin notifying his contacts before the week is out. 'You leave it to me,' Mr. F. told him."

"Now that is very charitable of Mr. F," I said with my head bent low, slipping the second sock over my mending-gourd.

"I think so," he said. By this time he had on his pajamas and was in bed reaching for his book on the nightstand. I watched him, out of the corner of my eye, flicking the pages of his ornately bound copy of *The Complete Adventures of Sherlock Holmes*, searching for the place where he had left off.

"I've never been successful in getting you to use a bookmark, have I?" I said, but he wasn't paying attention, he was too intently flicking.

"Mmm?"

"Never mind," I said. Having found his place, the room became quiet. I continued my darning, listening to the peaceful chirping of the cool-weather crickets.

"Sweeheart?" he said, talking into the pages of the open book held upright on his chest.

"Hmm?"

"Sweetheart, must you do that now?"

"Well..." I secured my needle and dropped the sock and mending-gourd into the basket. I got out of my chair and looked into the dark eyes of my clean-shaven husband, eyes that peeked over the pages of his book. And I said, "Can you think of anything better I could be doing?"

"As a matter-of-fact I can," he said, and smiled. And we both laughed.

Chapter Twelve

Our Mystery Guest Arrives

*It is never too late
to give up your
prejudices.*
Henry David Thoreau

Emma and I paced ourselves so that by Friday we were prepared for our guests. Blackberry Inn was ready. Even the windows were clean and sparkling. Friday's supper was a simple country spread, served family-style. All the leaves had been put into Emma's long table, making it longer still, and every chair was taken. I was dismayed at how fast the farm cheese disappeared, but before the meal was over I had a large bowl of my juicy fried apples set out to fill in the breach. Michael had registered all the guests but one. Mr. Fortesque and his lady were late. Mr. Fortesque was never late. Mindful of this, Emma kept some food aside. I was already jittery with suspense and their tardiness made me more so.

Donald, to whom had been given the task of delivering bags to their right rooms, answered the front door. "Mom, Mr. Fortesque's here," he announced, loud enough for both his dad and me to hear. It took only one nervous glance at Michael for him to make haste to come to my side. Removing his hat, Mr. Fortesque stepped inside behind his lady. Donald, Michael, and I stood like a row of manor house servants to greet them, I in my stiffly starched pinafore. But Mr. Fortesque softened the scene by addressing us warmly, calling us his "dear friends." The lady was younger than I expected and had an unworldly beauty. There was a touch of naiveté in her countenance. I thought I had seen her somewhere before. In less than a minute I remembered where. She was the strawberry blonde I had seen in Tony's shoe shop, the one who had been keeping up to date with the latest style in high heels. Come to think of it, wasn't it the doorstep of the shoe shop where we had met Mr. Fortesque that day?

Mr. Fortesque put a gentleman's hand on my shoulder and said, "Carol, Michael, I'd like you to meet my niece, Miss Siobhan Pinkette." Miss Pinkette's smile turned into a grin. She took a step toward Michael. She looked up at him, squinting, and said slowly, "I've seen you somewhere before."

In the midst of her recollection I spoke up. "We were in Tony's shoe shop not too long ago, and I remember seeing you there."

"Isn't that funny?" she said, still looking at Michael. Then she turned to me and said, "Well, I'm very happy to meet you. My uncle has told me all about you and this place," she said.

Michael said, "This is our son, Donald. May he take your bag upstairs? I'll take your coat."

"You're in room five," Donald told her. "It's the blue room."

"Bob and Dora probably keep early hours," Mr. Fortesque said, "I don't wish to impose my hours upon them. I'll introduce Siobhan to Mrs. Cook, if I may, and then I ought to be going."

"Oh, but you must be hungry. Won't you stay for a bite to eat first?" I asked. "We've saved something for you in the kitchen."

He gave in. "It certainly smells good."

"The dining room is full," I had to tell them. "Would you mind sitting in the kitchen, or should I bring your plates into the sitting room?"

"The kitchen, by all means," Mr. Fortesque briskly answered. "Come this way, Siobhan." Placing a gentleman's hand on her back, he guided her forward and ushered her through the large sitting room.

I overheard her comment to her uncle as they passed the wide hearth, "Ooh, that fireplace is romantic, isn't it?"

"Indeed," he responded.

Michael, his head hidden inside the doors of the hall wardrobe, snickered as he hung up the coats. "Shh, they'll hear you," I said.

"You like surprises, don't you?" he snickered some more. It was his way of telling me, "I told you so."

"I know; I admit I am silly sometimes."

"That's an understatement."

"What's so funny?" asked Donald, as he came down the stairs.

"Oh, nothing," I said, and darted off toward the kitchen.

~~~

Even with her arms full of a heavy stack of dirty dishes, Emma glowed with more than her usual radiant hospitality upon seeing Mr. Fortesque and Miss Pinkette enter the kitchen. She placed her stack beside the sink and I handed her a dishcloth for her hands. After introductions were made, she held one of Miss Pinkette's hands and gave it a few pats while taking a moment to chat.

"They're eating in here," I informed her. Emma immediately seated niece and uncle at our messy kitchen table as if it were the best table at an upscale hotel. I was still clearing away its accumulation of stray dishes and bowls and taking them to the sink. The sink was Darby's station. He washed anything and everything as the steady flow of dishes was brought to him. His washing was a loud masculine affair involving the elbow grease of a wood splitter. What he lacked in quiet he made up for in speed and thoroughness. I hoped the noise and commotion would not create an unappetizing atmosphere for our kitchen diners. When the table was wiped clean, Emma covered it with a gingham cloth.

"How quaint," niece said to uncle.

My private assessment was that they would only nibble. But I was privately put to shame. The opposite proved to be true. They consumed their food with hungry momentum, pleasant conversation, and polished manners, oblivious to Darby's noisy dishes.

Miss Pinkette watched me from the corner of her eye as I scurried back and forth from kitchen to dining room, clearing away the last of the supper dishes and serving dessert. Emma had the coffee ready. On the way to the dining room she stopped in her tracks; with two hands firmly grasping her heavy coffeepot, she lifted her chin to my ear. "Miss Pinkette is trying to get your attention, dearest."

"Mrs. Weaver, I enjoyed my meal immensely. How do you make food taste so good?"

"Country sunshine and country rain give Appleton's food its flavor," was my reply. "I did nothing out of the ordinary." I meant every word.

"Delicious," she added, licking the last forkful clean, placing it on her plate, and fingering her napkin with confident femininity.

Mr. Fortesque seemed pleased with himself for having invited his niece. After an offering of his own carefully chosen words of appreciation, he said, "I must be off. I'll see myself out. Good night, Mrs. Cook."

Emma had an empty sugar bowl in her hand which needed refilling but she plunked it down next to the canister, saying that she needed to see Mr. Fortesque to the door. She pretended to be cross with him. "Just because we live in the country doesn't mean we throw caution and courtesy to the wind," she said.

He responded with suavity. "Far be it from me to ever be the cause of that, Mrs. Cook." Emma handed me her apron and graciously escorted her gentleman guest to the front door.

Seeing the dining room empty, Michael urged Emma and me to leave the remainder of the cleaning to Darby and him. Rather outspokenly, Darby said, with Irish inflection, "Be off with you, now." Donald was sweeping the floor. Following suit, he protested, "Excuse me, but you're in the way." We obeyed.

Some of the guests had already gone upstairs. A few sat languidly with full stomachs in the sitting room's glowing firelight, sharing less energetic conversation than had been shared in the dining room. Miss Pinkette was sitting beside Emily, taking such a keen interest in Colleen's paper wardrobe that she was drawing a dress on a piece of scrap paper. I immediately liked her, and sitting across from her was glad I was wearing my new shoes. Emma joined us.

"I so like Mr. Fortesque's new suit, don't you?" I said, welcoming a response.

Miss Pinkette spoke up, "'Uncle Ian,' I said, 'your suit will hang on you in tatters before you buy a new one. Let me help you find one that's more complimentary.' It was our standing joke because all the other times I'd offered, he'd shake his head and say he was far too busy for such things. I thought he'd never take me up on it. But finally, he did."

"Your taste is impeccable," Emma praised, "The suit is quite a handsome one, a perfect shade for your uncle, and a perfect fit, too." The compliment was meant for Miss Pinkette but it could have referred to Mr. Fortesque just as well.

I waited a few minutes for Colleen's new dress to be finished, and then ushered Emily up to bed in my new shoes that, at the end of a day whirling in activity, suddenly felt too tight.

Chapter Thirteen

Speaking the Truth in Love

*Never apologize
for showing feeling.
When you do so,
you apologize for
the truth.*

Benjamin Disraeli

Emma left the house at dawn on her bicycle as she and the Goslin sisters were helping to supervise the men who were setting up the enormous copper kettle over an open fire on the village green. The cider in the pot would be at a boil by the time folk arrived to add their apples. I was up early, too, and in the kitchen mixing batter for six dozen apple butter muffins—three dozen for Blackberry Inn, three for the church fund. I used up the cellar's last remaining jars of apple butter from the previous year's festival. The tang of the apple butter, the extra cinnamon, nutmeg, and clove, and the buttermilk had made them a favorite muffin of my childhood. A return of the cooler air of autumn and the availability of garden food makes me enjoy cooking in autumn better than any other time of year.

When I picked up my recipe card to return it to its box, I noted that it was written in my mother's hand. It was one of her many gifts to me after I married. I even remembered the day it was given. I missed her.

I sat down on the kitchen stoop, waiting for the timer to ring, surveying the yellow maples. A spotlight of low morning sunrays made the leaves gleam as bright as the yellows and golds in our church's stained glass window. I remembered the joy on the faces of my parents on Apple Butter Day. "They'll never know this child," I thought sadly, placing a hand on my belly, "and this child will never know them." Then I crossed my arms in front of me when a chilly breeze blew my way, for the sun's rays were deceiving.

"Good morning," Michael said in greeting. He sat down beside me, his eyes taking in the same gleaming sunrays. I enjoyed our quiet talks on the kitchen stoop, and wished we had more of them, and more time that morning to linger there together. "The children are dressed in what you put out for them," he reported.

"Thank you," I said.

"You look pretty today," he said.

"Thank you," I said again. I was more contemplative than talkative.

"A penny for your thoughts?" he asked. He took a penny out of his pocket, took my hand in his, and placed it in my palm.

But I brushed my thoughts aside. "A penny saved is a penny earned," I said, making a fist with it.

"And we've earned a pretty penny this weekend for Emma and ourselves," he said.

"That's good, because we'll need some in the apple butter."

"Is that what the recipe calls for?"

"The pennies keep the butter from sticking to the bottom of the pot," I said. I left him to brood over his new bit of country knowledge while I got up to answer the kitchen timer's ring.

Mr. Fortesque drove up. He had come to take Miss Pinkette to Bob's, as she had been invited to breakfast with them there. Our other guests all headed off to the festival. We were next. When Michael pulled our car up we all climbed in—Darby in his fisherman's sweater, I in my calico, a broad-brimmed hat, and old shoes. The children, though purposely underdressed, were neat, clean, and presentable.

The village of Appleton was bustling. As Michael parked our car at the edge of the green, Emily's eyes became round with apprehension. I encouraged her, saying, "Look, here come Seth and Sarah." They appeared out of a small crowd and found what they were looking for—our car and their friends, who were very happy to see them.

"Yes, you may go off," I told them, "but check in with us from time to time. We'll be near the kettle mostly."

"I'd like to be with Emily during her pony ride," Michael instructed Donald.

"Yes, Dad," Donald said.

I watched them walk into the crowd. Sarah intuitively took Emily's hand in hers. The gesture was sweet. I thanked God for friends. Sarah was used to being the youngest sibling in her family, yet being one year older than Emily put her in the position of looking after her younger friend. My girlhood sampler with the words, "Be ye always kind and true," came to mind. It seemed that Sarah's conscience was being trained in the same virtues.

The kettle was in the very center of the green. Emma, cheeks plumped by her sunny grin, waved when she spotted us. "Here's some pennies for the kettle," I told her.

She opened her palm. "Oh, good. We'll see that you get them back. Your mother always loaned us the pennies at festivals past," she said.

"Yes, I remember," I said. "It's a perfect day for making apple butter, isn't it?"

"Perfect."

Folk knew to step up to the kettle to take a turn at stirring which had to be constant. Traditionally, older children did the lion's share of the stirring and looked forward to the socializing. Emma was giving Michael a lesson in stirring when Mr. Fortesque and Miss Pinkette stepped up to the kettle.

"Hello, Miss Pinkette," Michael said.

"Please call me Siobhan," she said. She was addressing me, too. While Michael stirred and Mr. Fortesque talked with him and Emma, Siobhan made polite conversation with me. She seemed truly inquisitive in addressing her questions.

"Apple butter is quite simple to make," I answered. "We use cider, apples, sugar, and some of the pumpkin pie spices. Soft apples are used, such as Maiden's Blush. A mixture of apples, grown in the community, are in the pot. Stayman, Winesap, Rambo, and Pippin make a prize-winning recipe."

"I've never heard those names before. How do you know when it's done?" Siobhan asked.

"When the butter is reduced to this mark," I pointed, "that has been cut into our long stirring stick. That's when we add the spices, because if spices cook too long, they lose their flavor. Appleton's secret ingredient is a very small amount of root beer flavoring. The old timers once added sassafras."

"Oh," she said, but just then a breeze sent the fire's smoke in her direction and she waved a hand across her face.

"Would you like to see our church?" I asked her.

"Yes, I'd like that," she answered.

The old church had never looked so colorful as we strolled across the lane. On that day the scene could have made a picture postcard. Our white church was boldly accented by a red-leafed maple on its left, a yellow maple on its right, the green grass of the lawn, and the bluest of blue skies above. I opened the doors, which were always unlocked.

When we stepped into the dark church—dark only in comparison to the bright outdoors—Siobhan commented, "What an unusual stained glass window—so many different golds and blues." I was about to tell her the story behind it when low voices coming from a pew off to the side stopped me. My eyes had adjusted to the dimness and I recognized the silhouettes of Pastor Bingham, Mr. Pease, and Darby. Their heads were bowed in prayer. Siobhan saw the men, too. Together we slowly turned on our heels and I closed the doors behind us. As we walked back to the green together, I entertained her with accounts of the venerable characters of our village, colorful descriptions bordering on fable.

<hr />

Back on the green I found Dora sitting beside the bake sale table spinning at her wheel. "It's to draw attention to the food," Dora said. "It was Michael's idea."

"Really?" I said.

"We're nearly sold out," she said. Siobhan and I chatted with her for a time and then I left to look for Michael. I found him walking beside Emily and the pony. He pointed me out, and when Emily spotted me, she raised a hand off the saddle for an instant, enough to give me a short wave while still taking care to keep her balance. She was all smiles.

While I stood watching, Mr. Fortesque appeared at my side. "Thank you for taking the time to talk with Siobhan," he said.

"She's a lovely young lady," I replied.

"I wanted her to meet you, and Mrs. Cook and Dora, too. It's one reason I brought her this weekend. She's been to finishing school, but she has more to learn. I think it's good for her to see how you ladies work willingly with your hands, how you watch over the ways of your household and reach out to the needy. Siobhan is too clothes-conscious. It would be good if she understood that strength and honor are the best clothing, more important than the latest fashions." His speech was sprinkled with phrases from Proverbs 31. I hadn't exactly "reached out" to the needy; rather I stumbled upon one. But Mr. Fortesque had a way of rendering me speechless. And he was doing it again. Perhaps I didn't hide my astonishment well because Emma, who was standing behind us, came to my aid. With her hand on my arm, she said, "Mr. Fortesque can be rather alarming, dearest. His stark sincerity has that effect on people." He gave Emma an inquiring glance, but she would not enlighten him.

"You are very kind," I said to him at last, sounding to my own ears like a character out of an eighteenth-century novel, but the words were not all politeness. They were sincere and what I truly thought of him.

———

Excusing myself, I retreated to find the place where I had left our picnic basket. Michael and Emily found me and sat on the blanket beside me. "Did you see me?" Emily asked. Though she knew I had, she was making doubly sure of it.

"Yes, and you rode so well. Was it fun?" I asked.

"Yes," she said. "Sarah rode one, too. Her pony was biggest. Don't you think mine looked like Merrylegs?"

"Just like Merrylegs," I told her.

Donald came bounding over, plopped down on the blanket and drew up his knees. He was peevish. In a huff he complained to his father, "I didn't win anything."

"Was that the only reason you took part in the games?" his dad asked. "Didn't you have any fun?"

"I suppose it was fun. Seth didn't make us fall in the three-legged race. It was all my fault." Donald said.

"He has more experience at this sort of thing," said Michael. "I'm sure he laughed about it. Am I right?"

"We laughed until our stomachs ached," he said. "Now I'm aching for food." This was spoken as he opened up the basket to dig rambunctiously inside it. I'd never seen him so wound up.

"Hold your horses," I said, and moved his arm out of the way so that I could serve the food.

"Sorry," he said.

While we ate, a pair of cousins, very different in age and size, started playing Yankee Doodle, one on the fiddle, the other on flute. I recognized the pair from our Memorial Day service. "We've never had music at Apple Butter Festivals in past years," I said to Michael.

"Do you like it?" he asked me.

"Is this your idea, too?"

"Yes," he said proudly. "It's good for business. See? The tourists think it grand. And I have bigger plans for next year."

"I like the music," I admitted. Meanwhile I kept an eye open for Darby. I had made some sandwiches for him the way he liked them, with farmer's cheese and extra mustard.

~⟡~

Pastor Bingham and Penelope came by with Seth and Sarah to give us their greeting. "The music is festive," Pastor said. Michael could only nod because his mouth was full. I had sliced the bread rather thickly.

Penelope said, "Thanks for making the muffins, Carol. It must be busy at Emma's this weekend. Michael told us the inn is full."

Pastor seemed to be searching for what to say. "It's good to see so many people out." Although he must have been making small talk for a good many years with new congregants such as ourselves, he was apparently still awkward at it. This is sometimes true of brilliant and studious men so I've heard. Their higher thoughts predominate. Therefore, it wasn't strange that my thoughts should wander to something Michael had said recently about pastors. He had said that it is character one ought to look for in ministers of God's Word, not personality. What I didn't know, at that moment, was that Pastor had come over to ask a rather big favor of us.

The children ventured off, Sarah once again taking Emily's hand. Her gesture reminded me to tell Penelope of my thankfulness for her daughter's watch care. I added how it brought to mind the words of my sampler. She seemed touched by what I said. The men's conversation was in the background. It was only when I sensed a definite change in the tone of their voices that I turned my attention so I could hear them.

"Therefore," Pastor Bingham was saying to Michael, "there's something I need to ask of you and your wife. Since Miss Crabtree will be away for several weeks, we'll have no teachers at all for a time. We wondered if Carol would substitute at the village school. You see, with our shortage of teachers I am teaching the high school ages and Penelope has had to start teaching the youngest students. In the middle of looking for new teachers, Miss Crabtree has had to leave the school temporarily to take care of her sick mother. Now we need a teacher for the middle grades, too, that is, until she returns." Pastor's eyes met mine as he continued, "We can pay you, Carol, but only a very small sum, as Miss Crabtree is still receiving a salary during her leave of absence."

Penelope added a positive note. "You'll only need to use the readers in part; otherwise you're free to teach what you like and how you like. That's what I do with the little ones." Evidently the village school was experiencing a crisis.

Michael gave the reply. It was calmly diplomatic. "You'll have our answer tomorrow." A look of relief came to the faces of the askers, and when they ran out of small talk they bid us farewell.

"He's given us much to consider, hasn't he?" Michael spoke soberly.

"Yes, he has," I agreed.

I spotted my brother and waved. He saw us and walked over to us. He was holding onto to his son, who looked like he wanted down.

"Put Jonathan next to me," I said. "He's missed a nap, hasn't he?"

Bob sighed, once released of his squirming bundle. "Yup."

"How are you holding up?" I asked.

"I'm holding up, Sis," he said. "I'm grateful for Michael and Donald's hands. Darby's been a big help, too."

"Oh?"

"He's tackling our woodpile," he said.

I sneaked a look at Michael, and he changed the subject, saying, "They're getting electricity."

"They are? How wonderful!" I exclaimed.

"Have to," Bob said. "The government's forcing us to pasteurize. So you see, selling my surplus is more important to us than ever this year." I was listening, but I was also scanning the gathering for Darby.

"Have you seen Darby?" I asked the menfolk. "He hasn't eaten yet."

"No," they both said.

"I should tell you, Sis, that I gave Dad's old Bible to Darby. He was asking me questions about the Lord, which I was happy to answer, but I thought it would be good, too, for him to get his answers straight from the Word." I was not shocked at hearing this. Rather, I felt the better for it. Whether it would have been an indiscretion to say what I had seen taking place in the church earlier or not, I decided to keep it under my broad-brimmed hat.

Chapter Fourteen

Solitary Tree Stump

How else but through a broken heart may Lord Christ enter in.
Oscar Wilde

At three o'clock, spices were added to the apple butter, filling the air with a wonderful aroma and signaling to everyone to have their jars handy. Once the butter was jarred, everyone packed up. Even our indefatigable Emma acknowledged that she was tired. Michael asked Benjamin to take her bicycle to the parsonage so she could come back in the car with us to Blackberry Inn. Emma and the children got out at the house, but Michael asked me to stay with him in the car. "Baths tonight," I reminded Michael, and he relayed the message to the children through the car window. Then we headed up White Tail Road to Darby's farmhouse.

An unmistakable figure was sitting on a solitary tree stump. He turned around and stood up when he heard the car. Feeling a pull on my heart, I said, "I'll talk to him."

"I hoped you would," Michael said in as tender a tone as I had ever heard from him.

Trudging through the high grass with Michael, I said quietly, "Poor Darby. First he was scandalously unpaid by Mr. McDuff and then he had his heart broken in two." I don't think I was ever sorrier for a man in my life than I was at that moment.

As soon we as we reached him, Darby said, "I hope you weren't offended by me leaving the party."

"Not at all," I said.

"I wanted to work on me house." He was idly rolling a stone in the grass under his shoe. "Elspeth used to sit here and dry her hair in the sun."

"It's just where I'd sit," I said.

He looked at Michael and said, "It's good of you to drive up here. I was going to make me way to Emma's house soon." Somehow I didn't mind hearing the phrase, "Emma's house" this time. It seemed such a silly grievance compared to Darby's troubles. He had news to share. "I had a talk with your priest, I mean, your minister. The people I talk to seem to know about God, so I thought I'd hear what *he* had to say." With sincere conviction he told us, "I love Jesus now. He earned heaven for me and made me a true Christian. It's *His* forgiveness I needed more than anyone else's. Me life is His."

He looked at me and said, "I'm happy, Carol. I'm praying that Mr. Fortesque will find Elspeth and that she'll come back to me. But whatever happens, I want to trust God." The sun was lowering in the sky and the glare made Darby squint. He hung his head down, averting his eyes from the glare, and rolled the stone under his shoe some more.

Michael tried to encourage him. "Your faith to believe wasn't your own. It was a gift from God. Pray for more faith, Darby. God doesn't do the walking for us, but He does give us the faith and desire to follow Him, and we learn to depend on Him in all kinds of circumstances."

Darby paused to think about this. Then he said, "The Irish have a saying: 'However tall your grandfather is, you still have to do your own growing.' Whatever the future brings is God's doing, isn't it? It's wrong to worry."

"Fear God and you needn't fear anything else," Michael concluded.

Darby seemed to be turning over Michael's last statement in his mind. Then he burst out, "I must tell Bob and Dora and Emma and the children that Jesus is my Savior, God, and Friend." He started for the car and Michael and I walked at his side.

It was so good to see his face truly bright. "They're going to be filled with joy when they hear it," I told him. "This is the best of news, Darby. We're very, very happy for you." He opened my car door for me and I found myself giving him a congratulatory hug. God can do wonders with a broken heart when we give Him all the pieces.

All the way home we cruised downhill in high spirits. Darby's first words about his conversion made me think of the chorus of a hymn we had sung the previous Sunday: "If ever I loved Thee, my Jesus, 'tis now." This hymn seemed to match Darby's sentiments exactly. Perhaps the grateful words of this hymn had had an influence on him. As I listened to Darby talk to Michael in the car, I thought I would sing it more meaningfully from that day forward.

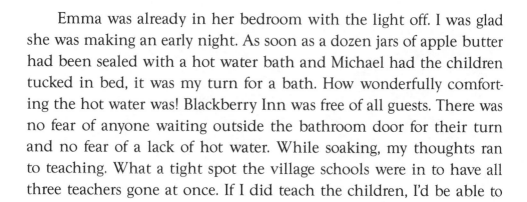

Emma was already in her bedroom with the light off. I was glad she was making an early night. As soon as a dozen jars of apple butter had been sealed with a hot water bath and Michael had the children tucked in bed, it was my turn for a bath. How wonderfully comforting the hot water was! Blackberry Inn was free of all guests. There was no fear of anyone waiting outside the bathroom door for their turn and no fear of a lack of hot water. While soaking, my thoughts ran to teaching. What a tight spot the village schools were in to have all three teachers gone at once. If I did teach the children, I'd be able to introduce them to beautiful paintings, to a greater understanding of what they read through Miss Mason's method of narration, get them to solve the mystery of arithmetic stories. I would even ask Emma if I could borrow her Victrola and phonograph records for a little music appreciation. My descriptions to Siobhan of those venerable characters of Appleton—those with early American skills—also came to mind.

When I entered the bedroom in my nightgown and robe, I found a fire lit and Michael standing at the window. The soft benediction of an early autumn evening filled the room with a peaceful glow. Michael stood gazing at the pink sky that was visible over the little hill of the cemetery. "I thought you might like to dry your hair by the fire," he suggested.

"Thank you," I said, recalling what Darby had said earlier about watching Elspeth dry her hair.

"I've given some thought to Pastor Bingham's request, and..." Michael started, still with his back toward the room. I should have

remembered that when his back is toward me while he's talking, that he is having difficulty finding the words he wants to say. But I wasn't sensitive to this. I was too filled with my own ideas.

"So have I, Michael," I interrupted. "I think it would be a wonderful opportunity to teach the children some things they might not learn otherwise. I'd be able to use some of the materials we have here and introduce the children to a wider scope of knowledge, and I could even get some of the country folk to demonstrate old-timey crafts..." I rattled on.

"Carol, I really do think..." he tried to interject.

But I was on a roll. "Mr. Candlewyck knows everything there is to know about beekeeping. He'd be glad to show us his apiary. Then there's always Mr. Pease and his horseshoeing. Mr. Percival, although most people think he's dim-witted, used to make marvelously sturdy brooms from broom corn, and Mrs. Percival made the creamiest goat's milk soap that..."

"Carol, I think teaching at the school would be too much for you. Sometimes I think you're *already* doing too much. Do Penelope and Pastor know you're expecting? I don't think so. And walking home in the rain on cold November afternoons would..."

"I'd wait at the school until you were off work at four o'clock."

Michael tried a different angle. "The phrase, 'a few weeks,' is ambiguous. There's no telling exactly how many weeks it'll be. You could be teaching until Christmas holiday if Miss Crabtree needs to stay away longer to care for her sick mother."

"Dora could talk to the children about shearing, carding, spinning, and dying wool."

Michael turned and looked at me face on. "Carol," he said in a louder voice and with more insistence. "You haven't heard a word I've said." This got my attention. He was in a rare mood. I stopped combing out my hair. "You have stars in your eyes."

"I do?" I said, and blinked.

"I mean it, Carol," he said, returning his gaze to the darkening sky. He sighed and said in a hushed tone, "If only you knew what I'm feeling inside." We were both silent while the flames in the fireplace crackled. I was afraid to speak, afraid to say the wrong thing. I had to admit to myself that I wasn't considering Michael's feelings at all, and was taken aback at how deep those feelings were when I heard what came out of his mouth next. "The saddest days of my life were those when our babies were born too soon," he said slowly, fixing his stare out the window.

"Really?" I said, bewildered. After another awkward moment of silence, I spoke to his back. "You never told me."

Touching the window glass with his finger, he said, "Look out there." I came to his side. "Have you ever noticed the tiny grave markers with 'Baby' on them? I don't want this baby to become one of those." Such intimacy made me start to tremble. I thought of Emma's babies, then I remembered my own. I remembered the pain and the shattered anticipation. I remembered how tiny and lifeless our babies had been, and how I had never gotten to cuddle them in my arms, look into their eyes, or say anything they would ever hear. Sorrow caught up with me and I could not stop it from surfacing. Michael turned around and wrapped me in his strong sympathizing arms.

Suddenly my lungs drew in gulps of air and I gave way to a burst of sobs. I buried my wet face in Michael's chest and a flood of hot tears rolled down my cheeks. His embrace welcomed me to share years of unexpressed grief. I was too good at stuffing my feelings inside and he knew this. I felt warm and safe in his arms. Eventually I stopped quivering. He took out a white handkerchief from his pocket and without a word placed it in my hand. Then he walked over to the fireplace, sat down in an easy chair, and did some more staring, this time at the small flickering flames.

That was when he told me another secret. With his eyes fixed to the flames, he said, "One day I pulled the car over in Bridgeton on the way to work, and had an unexpected cry. I assumed you'd had yours, sweetheart. But tonight I see I was wrong."

"Michael, you're right. They'll have to find another schoolmarm. I was getting too carried away." I finished drying my tears on his handkerchief and lay down on the bed because my head hurt. "I love you," I spoke across the room to him.

He turned and looked at me with a serious expression, and said, "I'll never stop loving you." It felt good to stretch out on the bed. The flickering light and the occasional crackling spark of our little fire radiated its soothing powers, and I began to relax. Michael sat in his chair, quiet and spellbound by the dancing firelight. I noticed that the windows were now black with night but I was too comfortable to get up and close the curtains. Then a little thump in my belly startled me. "He kicked," I said.

"He did? Where?"

"Right here." Michael came and stood next to the bed and I guided his hand to the spot. We waited a few moments in stillness. Then we felt another fluttery thump.

"That's him all right," Michael said. "He wants you to know he agrees with me."

Before the night ended we talked over my idea of teaching whoever wished to come to Blackberry Inn for morning lessons only, unless we were going on an outing in the community to learn about colonial occupations. It was the plan we settled upon so that I could be a help to the school but in a more limited way than was proposed. Michael felt comfortable about this compromise. The next day he would present it to Pastor Bingham, who was the chairman of the board of directors. We fell into a deep and peaceful sleep.

In the morning we decided to tell the children about the baby because we wanted them to know before we told Pastor and Penelope. We entered their room early. Perched on the end of Emily's bed, Michael gave the children the news. As soon as he did, Emily moaned, "But now I won't be the baby anymore! Who will love me?" I hadn't known that she thought of herself that way, especially at her age. I put an arm around her.

"Everybody takes a turn at being a baby," Michael said. "I was a baby once." She found the idea a funny one and it seemed to satisfy her.

"And we will always love you and Donald as much as the baby," I told her.

My Jesus, I Love Thee

My Jesus, I love Thee, I know Thou art mine.
For Thee all the follies of sin I resign.
My gracious Redeemer, my Saviour art Thou,
If ever I loved Thee, my Jesus, 'tis now.

I love Thee because Thou hast first loved me,
And purchased my pardon on Calvary's tree.
I love Thee for wearing the thorns on Thy brow.
If ever I loved Thee, my Jesus 'tis now.

I will love Thee in life, I will love Thee in death,
And praise Thee as long as Thou lendest me breath;
And say when the deathdew lies cold on my brow,
"If ever I loved Thee, my Jesus 'tis now."

In mansions of glory and endless delight,
I'll ever adore Thee in heaven so bright.
I'll sing with the glittering crown on my brow,
"If ever I loved Thee, my Jesus, 'tis now."

Chapter Fifteen

Welcome to the Fold

Never be afraid to trust an unknown future to a known God.

Corrie ten Boom

Not all the congregants accepted Darby into the fold equally. That Sunday I watched from my pew those in front of me who talked behind hands while peering over shoulders. The same congregants made sure to hold Darby at arm's length. I hoped he wouldn't notice, and I don't think he did, as he already had his own circle of friends. In fact, we had reason to have a closer kinship to him as a result of his commitment to Christ.

When Michael and I told Pastor Bingham in what way I was willing to help, he took it as a blessing. He would begin spreading the news that very day for a Tuesday starting date, which gave me one day to prepare. Pastor handed me a set of readers and Miss Crabtree's attendance record book. Then Michael privately shared the news that I was expecting. Pastor and Penelope congratulated us warmly.

Emma was so happy about Darby's newfound faith that a welcome-to-the-fold party was planned for that very day. She invited the small circle of friends: the Binghams, Bob and Dora, and Mr. Pease. I was concerned, because the apple butter making had used up so much of her energy. I expressed my concern to her. She reassured me, however, that a late afternoon party was early enough in the day to let her get "early to bed," and late enough in the afternoon to give her plenty of time to bake a cake *and* have a lie-down. "Besides, I have a craving for carrot cake," she said. Hospitality was second nature to her, more so than with anyone else I knew.

I had just rolled up my sleeves to the elbow to wash the midday dishes when I heard talking in the dining room. I walked down the hall to spy it out. "What's this?" I asked Donald. He was carrying a very small chair.

He said, "Grandma told me to bring a set of table and chairs down from the attic for Emily and Sarah. I think it's for their dolls."

Emily was holding her stuffed dog and bear. "Sarah is bringing Raggedy Ann," she said. I guessed that Emma had also sparked the idea for a little girl's tea party.

"Oh, how nice," I said.

Back in the kitchen Emma was grating carrots for her cake while the butter sat out to soften. I set to work on a small stack of dishes. "No help needed," I told Darby when he poked about the kitchen. "Relax for a change. It's Sunday, and a special Sunday at that."

"Mr. Pease is bringing the rabbit fur with him," he told Emma. "He's going to show me how to soften the skins with oil, now that they've been scrapped and cured in that fizzy liquid he calls weed killer."

Emma enlightened me. "We're going to make Elspeth a rabbit fur muff."

I thought muffs were more for the horse and buggy days, but Darby said that in his wife's childhood she had always admired the well-to-do ladies in town who had worn them. It would be a dream come true to have a fur muff of her very own. "I want to impress her. I have to win her back, Carol. That's a man's job, isn't it?"

"I suppose it is," I said. "I'm sure she'll love it, especially if Emma's going to make it. She's an excellent seamstress."

Standing in front of her bowl of flour sifting in the baking powder, Emma said, "We'll need more rabbits." She broke the news to Darby gently, without looking up from her sifting. "It takes more skins than one might think to make a good piece of fabric."

Darby, however, was not put off by Emma's requirements. "Not a problem," he said. He was adept at capturing small furry critters of all kinds.

<hr />

It was a dismal November day outdoors, which made the house shadowy. After Emily finished setting up the little table to her satisfaction, we spent a cozy hour, just the two of us, in my bedroom making calico yo-yos. Our collection of them was growing. Michael, Darby, and Donald were playing a game of Chinese checkers in the living room. Emma kept her word and took a nap.

<hr />

The party was pleasant. For the first time we heard Darby laugh. He accepted a third slice of cake when it was offered, and then adjourned to the sitting room with the men. We ladies remained seated but regrouped at one end of the long table, chatting on feminine topics, while Emily and Sarah sat at their little table. They were living in a world of make-believe, a world they had created from what they had seen and heard adults do, and from their storybooks.

Dora told me that she found the girls' make-believe sweet and amusing. Perhaps she was gratified that her own example might have had some influence on the creativity. I was sure it had. She let Jonathan down and he crawled over to the girls. The little table was the perfect height for him to pull himself up at one corner, and I was surprised to see him standing. His legs were a little wobbly, but he seemed pleased with himself and more content at that moment than in the high chair or on his mother's restraining lap. Dora kept a watchful eye for any mischief he might cause. "Babies are babies for such a very short time," Penelope commented. We all agreed. Emma added, "Yes, but I can still feel the arms of my two year old around my neck."

Out in the sitting room I spoke with Mr. Pease about sharing his knowledge of horseshoeing with the children and giving a demonstration. He said he'd be glad to, but he didn't expect the children to learn anything new. I reminded him that as the motorcar and tractor continued to replace the horse at a remarkable speed, children might not be as familiar with the trade as they once were. He conceded at last, fearing I might be correct and that soon the horse would be replaced altogether—perhaps even in his lifetime.

I also spoke to Emma about borrowing her Victrola for the children's music appreciation lesson. "Let's play something for the party right now," she said brightly. The Victrola was normally kept in her bedroom, but she carried it out and placed it on the gate leg table in the sitting room. While she was looking through her collection of records for something lively, I talked to Pastor and Penelope. I started to explain Miss Charlotte Mason's opinions on the presentation of "pictorial art," as she called it.

My voice must have been laced with conviction because little by little everyone in the room became quiet and listened attentively to my speech. Pastor nodded in the pauses. "Art training should proceed on two lines," I said. "The child should learn both to express himself and to appreciate, and his appreciation should be well in advance of his powers to express what he sees or imagines. His appreciation should go beyond the pictures of his storybooks. Even a young child can learn to look at real art. Miss Mason believed that the child's mind would accommodate itself to what is put in front of him. I believe that what holds true for pictorial art also holds true for music. A child's listening should be well in advance of any powers he might have to play an instrument. Or what his uncle can play on piano, for instance," I added. This was my sister-to-brother jab. Bob was the piano player of the family.

"I beg your pardon," Bob jested.

"What about the church organist?" chuckled Mr. Pease, who knew he sometimes played off tempo.

"Well spoken, dear," said Emma, always the encourager.

"What you say is interesting," said Penelope.

Pastor added, "Yes, quite interesting. I understand what you're saying, Carol. Children are educated in the language of their culture and the stories and poetry written in that language, but they typically learn so little about their cultural heritage in music, art, and architecture, don't they? Therefore, what you say gets me thinking. It used to be that a student had to travel to Europe to experience such culture, yet with the right materials we can give children a piece of it here at home, can't we? Perhaps not so much in architecture, but in music and art, we can."

The phonograph record started revolving, which made Donald, Seth, and Benjamin stop playing jacks on the wooden floor and come over to watch and listen. Curiosity also drew forth Emily and Sarah from the dining room, their stuffed friends under their arms. We all enjoyed previewing what I might play for the children during the weeks to come.

One friend was missing: Mr. Fortesque. At the close of our party we had a time of prayer and praise. We were all thankful for Darby's new faith. A deep-felt prayer of supplication was given on Darby's behalf, that Mr. Fortesque would locate his family. A prayer spoken for me set off butterflies in my stomach. I was embarking upon a new adventure and hoped that I hadn't bitten off more than I could chew. It is good to have a vision, but carrying it out is another matter altogether. Michael squeezed my hand during that prayer.

With gratefulness for the occasion, Darby stood at the doorway shaking hands and seeing everybody off one by one with a wave. He dawdled, while the wide-open door filled the foyer with a draught of chilly air. I saw why. His gaze was fixed on Dora carrying Jonathan down the path to the truck. It's funny how a mother, especially, is gifted with eyes in the back of her head, because Dora intuitively twisted around in the middle of the path to give one last wave to Darby. His wave in return was a melancholy one. It occurred to me that what he saw wasn't Dora and Jonathan at all, but a flashback of Elspeth and Andrew walking out of his life.

Chapter Sixteen

Children of Blackberry Inn School

A man should hear a little music, read a little poetry, and see a fine picture every day of his life, in order that worldly cares may not obliterate the sense of the beautiful which God has implanted in the human soul.
Johann Wolfgang van Goethe

Monday morning brought a welcome change of pace. I enjoyed the calmer routine of the house, sitting with the children first in the quiet sitting room for reading and narration, then at the table in the library for writing, drawing, and arithmetic. Geraldine was making a good start on the bed linen from our houseful of guests over the weekend.

All that could be heard emitting from behind the closed door of the kitchen was the low hum and rumble of the washing machine.

We finished our chapter on Sir Walter Raleigh and the first English colonists. This meant I could begin reading about Pocahontas and the settlement of Virginia to our expected group of children the following day. While Donald and Emily did their numbers, I chose our new painting by Peter Graham titled "A Rainy Day." It achieved what Chesterton said of Graham's work in general, in that it displayed "a remarkable feeling for the beauties of atmospheric effect." I guessed the children would take an interest in the boy in the picture trying to control an unruly horse and they did. It would be this painting that I would also display to the class on Tuesday. I decided to also save our science lesson on the history of clocks and timekeeping for Tuesday.

Just before lunch Donald willingly retreated into his room to read his John Eliot. He kept Rudyard Kipling's *Jungle Book* by his bedside, but he knew that that was reserved for times of leisure reading. Since Emily was still so very new to reading chapter books, I allowed her a storybook for lesson hours. She and I sat close together on the sofa with *Winnie-the-Pooh* open on her lap. I asked her to read to me some of what she had already read silently to herself. She enjoyed sharing it with me, and together we giggled at the antics of Christopher Robin's silly bear. When she closed the book it crossed my mind how different tomorrow would be.

That afternoon I overheard Emma answering a telephone caller. "Yes, the autumn color will be at its peak...So that's two for Friday evening?...Your name, please. Make a right at Peddler's Junction off the main highway. After three miles you'll see a large red barn on your left on the corner of Mill Creek Road. Make a left onto Mill Creek, another left on Paw Print..." That telephone call heralded the approach of another busy weekend at Blackberry Inn.

～～

"Good morning, sleepyhead. Today's your first day of school, remember?" Michael said, waking me. He was dressed for work. I had overslept. He gave me a kiss good morning and headed downstairs. I heard one of my cardinals tweeting and went to the window. A glimmer of red on a branch perked me up. "Hello," I said. I also noticed a light frost on the tips of the grass below. I opened the window an inch so the cool air would revive me further. Except for the cardinal's isolated tweets, it was remarkably quiet outside.

By the time breakfast was over, the earliest sunrays had melted the frost into dewdrops. Frosty weather always turned my thoughts to what I had "put by" and I was glad our cellar was full of bottles of preserves as well as the apples Darby and Donald had gathered. Darby's rigging system had produced a greater yield from the old apple trees than Emma or I had thought possible. Three bushels of the not-as-nice apples remained in the corner of the kitchen, waiting to be turned into jars of applesauce.

Emily said over her oatmeal, "Mommy, Donald says we're goin' punkin' pickin' at Uncle Bob's."

"Dad said he'd take us after work tomorrow," Donald revealed.

"I always look for the heart-shaped pumpkins," I said. "And it's 'pumpkin pick-ing,'" I corrected Emily. She repeated my enunciation. I decided not to fuss, however, with correcting any of the students when a country colloquialism presented itself. Correcting my own children in private was enough fuss.

An early knock at the kitchen door made the oatmeal stick in my throat so that I had to swallow twice. Donald answered the door, and in walked our first students, Seth and Sarah. Seth said politely, "Good morning, Mrs. Weaver. We've been very much looking forward to your lessons. Our mother said it would be a privilege to come here. She told us a little about what you teach. It sounds swell. Where should we hang up our coats?" He held both his coat and Sarah's in his arms. I was flattered by his manners. Seth apparently was an agile talker.

One quick glance at the muddy floor and my floor-boy agreed with me that the children should take off their shoes in the kitchen. He would answer the door and tell our new students what to do. Emily was in charge of the coats. Soon children stepped into the kitchen, some chuckling about the things children chuckle over, some apprehensive. One little girl was spindly-limbed and looked too young for my lessons. I wanted to braid her flyaway hair. Her name was Lydia. Despite appearing undernourished, as it turned out she proved an attentive little pixie, and when questioned always answered directly in a voice as quiet as a whisper. A boy with a fuzzy orange cowlick straggled in forty-five minutes past the hour and missed Picture Study.

I was told that B.J. lived "up the ridge." He carried with him the aroma of his morning chore. My educated guess was pigs. I was relieved no giggles were made about him. The children were evidently used to it.

Emma's long table in the dining room was put to good use. After roll call I explained to the children about Picture Study. "A Rainy Day" was propped up on the mantelpiece. Following my direction the children walked up in groups of threes to study it up close. They found this amusing. The writing of their descriptions would come later in the week.

I read aloud the first chapter of the life of Pocahontas and called on Donald to stand up and demonstrate narration. I was pleased that our history book accomplished just what Miss Mason said a good history should, that is, to

> *purl along as pleasantly as a forest brook, 'tell you all about it,' stir your heart with the story of a great event, amuse you with pageants and shows, make you intimate with the great people, and friendly with the lowly.*

The right book makes all the difference.

I knew the children's readers contained few if any humorous poetry, so to keep our first day light I read a poem from *My Book House*: "The Acorn and the Pumpkin" by La Fontaine. The children chuckled. When I asked for volunteers to read the poem out loud, hands were raised. Hence they heard the poem repeated four more times. As it increased in familiarity, it seemed to increase in delight.

Next I began our science study of the development of clocks and time-telling. I called on Seth to narrate the paragraphs I had read aloud to the class. I thought as an older student and a proven orator, he would be a candidate for narration. His frequent starts and stops told me that this factual material was a bit of a challenge to put into words smoothly. I was inclined to help him along, but reminded myself of what I had read the night before,

> *that it is very important that children be allowed to narrate in their own way...A narration should be original as*

*it comes from a child—that is, his own mind should have
acted upon the matter it has received. Narrations which
are mere feats of memory are quite valueless."*

I would need to select some simpler readings for the younger students, who were entirely new to narrating. My *Book House* had good material for this. Volume Four had a tall tale about Paul Bunyan and the legend of Johnny Appleseed, which I bookmarked for later in the week. The poem, "The Planting of the Apple Tree," by William Cullen Bryant, would be another good one.

To prevent any slowing momentum of the morning, I informed the children that after they had finished their silent reading in their readers, they could take out their snacks. Then I would play a phonograph record while they drew a picture to illustrate our poem for the day. The anticipation did, indeed, encourage them. In the future I would require drawings from history and science.

During silent reading, Sarah—who was seated beside Emily—was curious about the illustrated pages of *Winnie the Pooh*. They were irresistible. It must have seemed incredulous that such a book would be deemed a schoolbook. "Would you like to read it when I've finished it?" Emily whispered to Sarah. After Sarah had read only a little of her reader, she began reading over Emily's shoulder. I wondered what I should do. For the time being I did nothing.

With my announcement of Friday's outing, an announcement that I would remind them of later in the week, I excused the class.

"Good-bye, Mrs. Weaver."

"See you tomorrow, Mrs. Weaver."

"Mom, I think they like you," Donald told me when all the children were gone. He seemed proud of this surmise.

"I'm glad," I said. "More importantly, though, I want them to like learning." I hoped that they had been duly impressed with the day's lessons and had gone away with some degree of new knowledge.

After lunch Emma leafed through a pile of back issues of *Liberty Magazine* that Mr. Fortesque had left in the living room for us. "Look, Carol. This issue has Michael's advertisement," she said, holding open the page. It read: "Blackberry Inn—for a country respite. Healthy supper served family style." The dates of the Apple Butter Festival and autumn's peak show of leaves were listed below.

"I'll have to ask Michael who penned the illustration of the house," I said. "It's pretty good." I took a copy of the magazine upstairs to read during my own brief "country respite" and tried to keep my mind off another house full of guests.

Chapter Seventeen

One Another

The government cannot create a rugged individual. God alone can do that. The government can only destroy one.

Drake Raft

The woodshed along side the carriage house was stacked daily with split wood. Darby filled his days with work all around Appleton. No longer needed at the canning factory, he did jobs for Bob, Mr. Pease, the Goslin sisters, and others—some for barter, and some for cash. He managed to fit in work on his own house before returning at the end of the day to Blackberry Inn, where he helped us in any way he could. I put my trust in Darby's rabbit hunting and planned two big pots of stew for Friday's guests.

Donald excitedly joined Darby on the hunt, returning not only with game but an interesting wild harvest. "Mr. O'Reilly asked me if

I knew where the gold daisies grew. I showed him that place by the fence and he pulled up the artichokes," he said.

"I know what this is," I said, looking at the small pile of orange-edged tree fungus. "I learned a little about mushrooms from my father. He called this type chicken-of-the-woods. But what are these?"

"Mr. O'Reilly said that they're wild parsnips," Donald told me.

"They should flavor our stew nicely," I said. I could see that Donald felt good about contributing to our supper. I simmered the rabbit, then peeled and cut the vegetables, both wild and domestic, and set them aside to be added later.

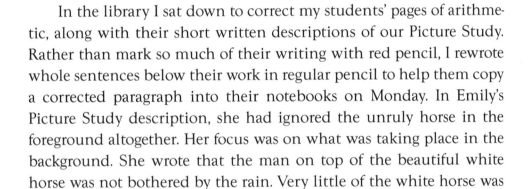

In the library I sat down to correct my students' pages of arithmetic, along with their short written descriptions of our Picture Study. Rather than mark so much of their writing with red pencil, I rewrote whole sentences below their work in regular pencil to help them copy a corrected paragraph into their notebooks on Monday. In Emily's Picture Study description, she had ignored the unruly horse in the foreground altogether. Her focus was on what was taking place in the background. She wrote that the man on top of the beautiful white horse was not bothered by the rain. Very little of the white horse was pictured because it was retreating, but Emily imagined it beautiful.

Donald and Sarah made inferences, too. Donald wrote that it was the boy's first day of his apprenticeship and that this was why he was having trouble with an unwilling horse. Sympathetic Sarah said the same horse had a stone in its hoof, thus excusing its behavior. I was not certain how much of a child's inference Charlotte Mason would allow. My reading of *Home Education*, however, had taught me to welcome a child's ability to reason and expand the powers of his imagination. If intelligent inference was what an artist's picture encouraged, I would make allowance for it with my students.

All week I read the same poem aloud, Longfellow's "Village Blacksmith." It was my favorite of all his poems. I read it at the start of our day and the end of it. On Friday I wanted to know how many could recite the first six lines by heart, and asked for a show of hands.

The children were puzzled. Donald was bold enough to ask if they were supposed to have memorized it.

"You may be unaware of it, but I think some of you have learned it just from my reading of it, and might like to give it a try. You might be pleasantly surprised. Seth, how about you?" I purposely hadn't mentioned memorization all week because I was trying an experiment based on the plan Miss Charlotte Mason had outlined in *Home Education*. Her plan was for very young children. I was trying my experiment with children somewhat older, but I thought the same theory would apply. Miss Mason claimed that without any wearisome verse-by-verse repetition, a child can learn a verse simply by hearing it over and again during the course of a week or so. As long as his mind is open and engaged, he will receive the impression, a stronger impression than if he has an aversion to the labor of committing something to memory. Having spent so many years closely working with children, Miss Mason discovered that children's minds are more able to readily take to forming beautiful images clothed in beautiful words when they are at ease. This facilitates their learning by heart.

Longfellow's "Village Blacksmith" proved to be the lyrical poem to accomplish this. It is a poem of beautiful images and beautiful words. Seth did well reciting it, and so did all the other children who volunteered willingly. I was especially moved when Lydia raised her hand for a try. Her voice was so quiet that I had to crouch next to her to hear her recite. Although her words were a whisper, and she ventured only the first two lines, it was flawless. But my biggest surprise was when my orange cowlick volunteered. B.J.'s colloquialisms would have perplexed anyone who hadn't been raised here in Appleton. Therefore, although his English was marred, he was perfectly understandable to me. I was happily satisfied with my experiment.

On Friday Emma came with us on our outing to Mr. Pease's stables. At my suggestion Donald handed an apple to each student as we headed out. The children welcomed the offer, despite the bumpy texture of the fruit's less than picture-perfect skins. Little Lydia held

Emma's hand during the walk, taking bites out of one of our most dimpled but juicy apples as she walked along. "I could use your help shepherding the children," I had told Emma earlier when she asked if she could assist me. They weren't an unruly bunch, but they could be talkative. I was concerned that they would ask Mr. Pease too many questions while he worked. It ended up, however, that he was only too flattered to receive such attention and esteem. Everyone set out for home after the demonstration. A note on the front door of Blackberry Inn invited any early guests to enter, as the door was unlocked, but when we returned no one had yet arrived.

I heard Michael shortly after we returned. He had come back just in time to register a middle-aged couple who had evidently pulled into the drive the same time he did. A little while later a gentleman arrived alone and Michael registered him. When they could be heard climbing the stairs, I walked unnoticed through the foyer and living room to the kitchen. It was time to add my vegetables and mix some biscuit dough, or should it be dumplings, I wondered? Dumplings, I decided, with a pinch of thyme and rosemary. The oven was large enough to fit three Dutch ovens, two of which I had found decorating the fireplace. When the broth had been reduced to a rich caramel color, I transferred it into the Dutch ovens to finish simmering. I would add the dumplings just before serving. While Emma and Emily set a pretty autumn table, another couple arrived.

I had kept my word to Dora about having her and Bob for supper when we were expecting guests. Greeting me that evening, she told me that Bob had had Darby's help to milk the cows. "So he's helping with the cows, too, now," I said, "How busy he's become." His help made it possible for Bob and Dora to linger at the table and share in the stimulating conversation.

The conversation turned out to be a regular round table of discussion. As the evening progressed, the men especially were free with their opinions. The discussion became a bit heated over coffee and dessert when someone brought up the topic of Roosevelt's New Deal. All of our guests had something in common: They were readers of Bernarr Macfadden's *Liberty Magazine* and were familiar with the pro-capitalist articles he wrote. (It was this magazine that had printed Michael's small advertisement about Blackberry Inn, to which they had all apparently responded.) One gentleman said, "Taxing one group of citizens to favor other groups goes against the beliefs of our Founding Fathers."

Emma was graciously outspoken. She said sadly, "The worst thing the president did was to destroy millions of dollars' worth of food while millions of our citizens are living on charity."

Bob could not contain himself on this point. He puffed out his thick moustache and said, "As a dairy farmer, I think it's intolerable. Because of some elaborate price-fixing scheme the government's playing at, milk is being poured into ditches and crops are going up in smoke. And yet people are still lining up in the streets across the country begging for bread and milk. What's happening to the backbone

of America? Thrift and self-reliance were what people lived by, not to be coddled and cared for by the government. It's always been family, church, and neighbors that provide support, encouragement, and accountability for as long as I can remember." My brother was patriotic, but I had not known him to be this vocal. Dora looked over at me and we shared a silent understanding across the table.

Michael said, "If the government weren't so involved in trying to fix things, this depression would be over a whole lot sooner."

The middle-aged man broke in, "F.D.R. should mind his own business and let us mind ours. The government's made a mess of things. How about the president's huge increase of the size of government, adding to the federal payroll, while at the same time growing the government in so many ways that it's in competition with private businesses like my own. My small business is so heavily taxed that I can barely keep the few people I have left on payroll."

"Disgraceful," said Michael. "It's maddening. Has any other president encouraged the passing of so much legislation known to be unconstitutional?" Once in a while Michael showed a small flame of fire under his unruffled demeanor.

Darby had the last word. "Whatever you say, I'm proud to be an American. I was sworn in just a few years ago. I'm a citizen. God bless America, my home, sweet, home.

Emma was the first to congratulate him. "Well done," she said.

"Here, here," the men said together, giving Darby a short round of applause. He stood up and bowed to his fellow Americans, then left to wash the dishes. That night Blackberry Inn sounded more like a public house than a country inn, though not a drop of liquor was served.

Emma and I followed Darby into the kitchen. A few moments later the telephone rang and Emma went to answer it. It was for Darby. When he returned to the kitchen he shared with us that Mr. Fortesque was doing all he could to find his family. "He told me that he is leaving no stone unturned and to keep me chin up," Darby said to us.

"That's right, you don't give up," Emma said, putting a hand on his back.

"I have enough money for paint to whitewash the cottage," he said. "I can start tomorrow after I do the wood." This fact cheered us up.

On Saturday morning we all awoke bright-eyed and bushy-tailed. The day was sunny, the air was breezy, and the sky was dotted with puffs of white clouds. I washed the tea towels and dishclothes, hung them on the line, and stayed in the garden enjoying the outdoors. A group of guests were gathered on the front lawn playing croquet. I liked watching Michael with Emily. It was Emily's turn to clean the chicken coop and she showed her dad what I had taught her. Afterwards Michael raked some leaves with her. The grass behind the vegetable garden was sprinkled with leaves, and there was just enough to cover him with a small pile. He lay on his back and Emily got to it. Then he gave her a ride in the wheelbarrow.

Donald sawed logs with Darby on the two-handled saw. They were finishing the job by stacking the logs in neat piles. Michael joined them in the stacking and Emily sat and watched the chickens. I sat peacefully putting the final touches on Emily's cardigan. I was pleased to find the perfect use for the opal shell buttons I had snipped off a worn-out piece of clothing two years earlier. I had been saving the buttons for just the right project. It is always elating to finish a piece of knitting. A gentle breeze blew the yellow-orange leaves that rustled overhead. They made dancing shadows on those that worked and played.

Nobody knew where Emma was. Soon after we had served our guests, she had vanished on her bicycle. I thought I had heard her say something about going to the Goslin sisters to bring back more goose down for the new mattress she was making for Darby. The Goslins had raised their pretty white geese since I was a girl. I remembered hearing my mother talk about their notorious gander. Rumor had it that he would nip the ankles of any stranger who approached wearing trousers, but accepted the visits of all in skirts. This was told to me years back as a possible explanation for why the Goslin sisters never married. A goose would a treat for Christmas dinner, I mused. My mind wandered upon such things while I sewed on the last button. It wandered some more as I considered making pumpkin pies for supper.

Just then Michael sat down beside me and said, "Here's my girl."

"Hi," I said.

"You look radiant this morning," he said.

"Thank you, I feel it. You look good yourself. Stacking wood agrees with you."

"Ha," he blurted out, and after a think, said, "I feel like walking. I'd like to see Appleton from outside of the car rather than always from the inside of it. Are you up to a walk? Emily says she knows a shortcut to town."

"If you don't mind walking around the piles in Mr. Pease's pasture, there're some things I need in town," I said.

"I'm game. You can be my guide," he grinned.

"But what about the guests? They're out front. And where's Emma?"

"She parked her bicycle against the carriage house a few minutes ago."

I looked up and spotted Emma's bicycle and then spotted her. "Here she is now," I said.

Emma came marching with purpose across the back garden. She was waving a letter in the air. "We found him!" she said excitedly. Darby and Donald stopped stacking as she approached them.

"Found who?" Darby frowned. Puzzled, he brushed the sawdust off his hands, for Emma was directing her announcement to him. She paused a moment, waiting for Michael and me to reach them. She had our full attention. Even the children wanted to find out what she was saying.

"The Goslin sisters gave me the address of Woodrow McDuff's daughter. She lives just a couple of towns away in Warren. I wrote this daughter a letter, Darby, explaining your situation. And she's just written me back with her father's address. Apparently he was stricken with an attack of diabetes and went to live with his son in Boston where he could be treated. Would you take us, Michael?" We were stunned, especially Darby.

"To Boston?" Michael asked.

"No, I'm sorry, to his daughter's in Warren. She's going to take the train from Forrest Green to visit him very soon." Emma held the letter open. "See? She says here that if we brought our letter of appeal to her, she would hand it to her father personally. It might add to its importance, she says. Isn't that fabulous, Darby?"

Darby was speechless.

So Michael responded, "I'd be happy to take you."

"Wonderful, Michael; good, good, good," she said. "I knew you'd say yes, so as soon as I got home, I went straight inside to telephone the number at the bottom of the letter, and it's all arranged. We're going to meet the daughter tomorrow after church. I wanted to have it all arranged before I told you."

Darby was still stunned by the news, but said, "I'm too messy to give a lady a hug, but I can shake your hand"—which he did. "T'anks," he said.

We had something new to pray about, something new to hope for.

Chapter Eighteen

Rain on the Roof

*Give me a stout heart to
bear my own burdens.
Give me a willing heart
to bear the burdens
of others. Give me a
believing heart to cast
all burdens upon Thee,
O Lord.*

John Baillie

By Saturday afternoon all the guests were gone. It was a good thing, too, since the sky opened up on Sunday in a big way. Just as we were ready to leave for church, the dark sky hurled its raindrops down in a fit of bad temper. I changed into my old shoes, and we waited at the door for a full ten minutes, hoping the pouring rain would let up, but then decided to make a mad dash to the car with our umbrellas. Along the way to church the windshield wipers did little to clear Michael's view of the road, a road that was becoming muddier by the minute. The car crawled.

During the worship service the thunder cracked. It seemed to roll over the roof of the church from one side to the other. Pastor Bingham paused now and again in his sermon to give it right of way. It would have been the perfect setting to preach from Revelation, but Pastor preached again from Proverbs. "A man's heart plans his way, but the LORD directs his steps" (Proverbs 16:9). He preached that it is wrong to adopt the secular notion that a thing called fate determines events or that God collaborates with fate somehow. He was giving us a bigger concept of God. *Everything* is determined by God's infinite wisdom and goodness, he preached. Our lives are not the product of fate or the result of capricious chance. We are guided by the all-knowing, all-loving, all-powerful, holy, and just God. Our days have been ordered for us. Our lives are in His caring hands. That's why one

Nigel Andreola

name for God is Providence. "For we are His workmanship, created in Christ Jesus for good works, which God prepared beforehand that we should walk in them" (Ephesians 2:10).

At the conclusion of the service I noticed Mr. Giles Thistlethorn talking with Darby. He was one of last week's whisperers. Maybe he had had a change of heart. Maybe that was his reason for being cordial. He could at least wear a smile. I talked with Mr. Candlewyck and then with Dora, both for only a minute or two on school matters, excusing myself abruptly when I saw Michael standing at the door. He had been canvassing for signatures from Pastor, Bob, Mr. Pease, and a few others in support of Darby's letter, and now he was watching for me. When our eyes met across the room, I nodded and collected the children for a prompt drive home.

It was still raining when we got into the car but not as hard as it had been, and the thunder was now distant. Along the drive I heard the crinkling of paper from the backseat and twisted around out of curiosity. Darby was unfolding a piece of paper, and without a word, he handed it to Emma. She read it and was repulsed. She said to Darby, "Giles Thistlethorn is beguiling. Shame on him! He should've been more tactful than to hand you this in church." She knew the man well.

"What is it?" Michael asked.

Darby spoke. "It says I'm to pay last year's back taxes on the house if I'm to live there, and that this year's taxes are due, too."

"Oh Michael, oh no," I said, so low that the rain on the hood of the car covered it from the ears of those in the backseat.

Michael said, loud and clear, "Well then, our letter to Mr. McDuff is more timely than we thought."

"Yes," said Darby in all meekness.

No one could hear Michael's melancholy sigh but me and our Emily, who was sitting between us. We knew Darby could not pay the taxes. Mr. Thistlethorn must have guessed this, too. He was not *only* doing his job. Based on Emma's reaction, he probably could not resist the satisfaction of being the one to deliver the very instrument that would get rid of an outsider. He could have delivered it personally to Blackberry Inn. Emma was right: Why the satisfaction of handing it to

Darby in church and on the Lord's Day? Was this his way of making a public statement? We would never find out. I stared blankly at the wet windshield in front of me until I became mesmerized by the cadence of the wipers. First I had a fretful heart. Then I empathized with Emma's exclamation of disgust with a private disgust of my own, "Shame on him!"

Although the heaviest rain clouds were gone, the sky was lead gray. The rain left the ground soggy and the trees without leaves. I was glad Michael didn't have to drive to Warren in a downpour. I made sure the travelers had blankets, sandwiches, cookies, and a Thermos of hot milky coffee for the car.

The house seemed too quiet and empty with just the children and me. Donald must have felt it, too. He asked, "Mom, can we hear the Chopin?"

"All right," I said not bothering to correct his "can" to a "may." We sat down to a game of Chinese checkers with Chopin's Nocturne playing in the background. Any other day I would have found it a soothing piece, but on that afternoon it sounded somber. Chopin's Raindrop Prelude (Op. 28, No. 15) played next. I always enjoyed its dynamics, but never before had it sounded so dark. Discouragement hung about me. The children sensed it. Donald was truly concerned. "Mr. O'Reilly is in trouble, isn't he, Mom?"

"Something like that," I said. I went on to tell the children about his predicament, ending with, "That's why we'd all like Mr. McDuff to pay what he owes Mr. O'Reilly, so that Mr. O'Reilly can pay the taxes he owes to the town. Then he can live in his house legally with his wife and little boy." I silently prayed that his faith would help him cope with yet another reason for worry and that Pastor's sermon would be taken to heart.

"Why do people have to pay taxes?" Donald asked. I was thinking how to answer his questions when Emily asked another.

"Where's his little boy?"

I told her that Mr. Fortesque was looking for Mr. O'Reilly's family because they were lost, that his little boy should be almost three years old, and that Mr. O'Reilly missed his family very much. Remembering Pastor's words about God's strategic care, I said, "Let's pray for them." I got up and lifted the needle off the record. Bringing our cares to our heavenly Father made us feel better, much better. And Chopin's next piece, his Waltz in E♭ Major, was brighter, with notes that bounced, played *vivo*.

Emily and I discovered that we needed to make only three more yo-yos that afternoon to have enough for Emma's pillow. When he saw that the yo-yo making had been quickly finished, Donald said, "Emily, I'll teach you how to be better at jacks." At that I went upstairs to sew the yo-yo pillow together. I had plenty of fabric for it and so I gathered a ruffle to put around the edge. I was feeling creative, so with the rest of the fabric I cut triangles. It occurred to me that, pieced with white, they would form a bright patchwork design. I was looking forward to seeing the inside of Darby's house clean and whitewashed. A patchwork pillow would make a nice housewarming gift to cheer Elspeth. I couldn't resist praying again—while my feet worked the treadle of the sewing machine—that the money owed to Darby would be given to him. "Please, dear Lord."

Chapter Nineteen

Providence

Old Brother Higgins built a shelf
For the family Bible to rest itself
Lest a sticky finger or grimy thumb
Might injure the delicate pages some.
He cautioned his children to touch it not
And it rested there with never a blot
Though Higgins tribe were a
troublesome lot.

His neighbor, Miggins, built a shelf
"Come children," he said, "and help yourself."
His book is old and ragged and worn,
With some the choicest pages torn,
Where children have fingered and thumbed and read.
But of the Miggins tribe I've heard it said,
Each carries a Bible in his head.

Anonymous

Monday morning brought children and mud into the house. Donald mopped up the mud during roll call, straightening the shoes in a long row to one side of the kitchen before Geraldine arrived. The painting I chose for Picture Study was "The Infant Samuel" by Sir Joshua Reynolds. It is not a picture of a baby, but a graceful composition of a young boy kneeling, with hands folded in prayer. Chesterton wrote that Sir Reynolds was "just as happy in portraying the innocent beauty of youth as the maturer qualities of age." He also wrote that in this painting "we have a combination of his qualities—the marked influence of the Italian School, the felicitous inspiration of the subject, and the beautiful coloring and dexterous workmanship which glorify the creations of his mind." I decided to read aloud chapter one of the first book of Samuel with some of what Miss Mason called "necessary omission." I had been impressed by what she wrote about children and the Bible. She said,

> *We are apt to believe that children cannot be interested in the Bible unless its pages be watered down—turned into the slipshod English we prefer to offer them.*

Further down the page she wrote:

> *We are probably quite incapable of measuring the religious receptivity of children. Nevertheless their fitness to apprehend the deep things of God is a fact with which we are called to deal prudently, and to deal reverently.*

She ended the section with touching words of wisdom:

> *But let the imaginations of children be stored with the pictures, their minds nourished upon the words of the gradually unfolding story of the Scriptures, and they will come to look out upon a wide horizon [where] persons and events take shape in their due place and in due proportion. By degrees, they will see that the world is a stage whereon the goodness of God is continually striving with the willfulness of man; that some heroic men take sides with God; and that others, foolish and headstrong, oppose themselves to Him. The fire of enthusiasm will kindle in their breast, and the children, too, will take their side, without much exhortation...*

I read the first chapter of Samuel in three parts, choosing three narrators. With only a week of practice, the children were already doing better than when they had first begun. They had become more comfortable about standing up in front of the class and putting my reading into their own words.

One late morning Bob took some time from his farming routine to drive Dora over to Blackberry Inn with her spinning wheel. She was going to give us a demonstration of an early American occupation. Bob held Jonathan part of the time but eventually let him roam, for it seemed that his son was eager to inspect each child who sat cross-legged on the sitting room rug. Dora started with the words of a nursery rhyme:

Cross patch, draw the latch,
Sit by the fire and spin:
Take a cup and drink it up,
Then call your neighbors in.

The children fingered the raw wool, the carded wool, the spun wool, and Dora's knitted lace shawl, while she gave them her story of "sheep to shawl," ending with a description of the different plants used for dying. Emily told Dora that she thought the yarn dyed with pokeberries was the prettiest. The girls took turns trying their skill at the drop spindle. The boys seemed more interested in the mechanics of the spinning wheel. When Seth asked a question that Dora was unable to answer confidently, Bob spoke up. He talked about the double drive band that fit into the groove of the wheel, the three-speed whorl with its three ratios, the drive belt tension, and the function of the ball bearings where the wheel is attached. As a result the children picked up some principles of elementary physics, something that Dora and I had not anticipated.

Our science subject that week was rocks and minerals. At my request, the children scavenged in their own neighborhoods for two different sorts of rocks and brought them to class. My fuzzy orange cowlick brought a pocketful. I made sure to give B.J.'s stones and pebbles the attention they deserved, happy that he had made a connection with the subject. This connection is what Charlotte Mason described as "forming a relation."

Our history chapter was about Henry Hudson's exploration. It noted that the Dutch on Manhattan Island named their settlement New Amsterdam until the English ruled and named it after the Duke of York. I drew a large map based on the small one in the book to give the children a geography lesson about the Hudson River and New York City.

One evening Donald asked me to make up some math story problems. "Okay, but I'd like your help," I told him. After he and I had done a half-hour of evening preparation together, I surprised my students the next day with a good many of them.

～～

Another Friday brought another outing. This time we all walked to Mr. Candlewyck's apiary in our wool sweaters. The air was chilly, but the sky cloudless, so the sun warmed our faces. Emma came along, too. Donald spoke to me in private. He told me that the children were expecting apples, so just as we had done before, we handed out one apiece for the walk.

We passed Mr. Pease out in his pasture carrying a bucket of water to his horses. He waved at us and the children waved back. When he saw us all with apples to our lips, he put down his pail, made a show of digging deep into a pocket, and pulled an apple out of it. He took a handkerchief out of another pocket to polish the apple, and then gave it a big first bite. The children all thought his little performance funny. "He's the baby of the family," Emma told me as we walked on. "And you know it's the babies that always act the clown."

"That figures," I said.

Taking a shortcut through some high grass, we arrived at the Candlewycks' back door. They looked happy to see us. We followed Mr. Candlewyck along a garden path to his hives, where he began his little speech. He told us that the cooler weather made the bees less active on the whole, but that the sunshine was perking them up a bit. His details of the life of bees—both in the meadow and in the hive, as well as how a bee makes honey—revealed his respect for God's creation. It was his enthusiasm that fixed the children's interest. When he showed us the inside of a hive, Emily stood well back. She had been stung quite recently and whispered in my ear that she didn't much care for bees. In his shed Mr. Candlewyck showed us how he spun honey out of the honeycomb to bottle it.

Mrs. Candlewyck showed us two different ways to make beeswax candles. One way of candle-making is to repeatedly dip the candles into a pot of heated wax. The other way is to pour the wax into molds. In both methods the wax has to be just the right temperature. "These tapers when lit will burn one inch per hour," Mrs. Candlewyck told us. I thought that that fact could be made into an interesting math problem. Emma chatted with Mrs. Candlewyck while together they dripped honey onto crackers and we all tasted a sample of the gooey golden sweetness before leaving. I was handed another crackerfull of honey, but gave it to Lydia. The apple blossom honey tasted so flavorful that I had to buy two dimes' worth, and was happy that it bought me quite a large jar.

Licking the ends of her fingers, Sarah said, "Delicious," as if she had never tasted honey before. Emily said to her friend, "If we eat any more honey, we'll get stuck in the door like Pooh Bear."

The walk back to Blackberry Inn took us through town. Darby saw us and joined up with us on the road. "I just came from the post office, and I have a letter in my pocket," he said. We could tell by his smile that its contents were favorable. Donald stood beside Darby and was interested, too. "It's from Mr. McDuff."

"Please, Darby," Emma said, "Tell us what he wrote."

"It's even better than I'd hoped," he said.

"You're being tantalizing. What is it?" Emma pleaded.

Darby put it plainly. "Not only did Mr. McDuff apologize for not paying my last wages and put a check in the envelope, but he has deeded me the apple orchard behind the house. He said that I purchased the house from him knowing there was steady work for me in his orchard. The house is of little use without the property behind it."

"That's wonderful, Darby," said Emma and I together.

"But will it cover the taxes?" I asked, more soberly.

Darby walked with a spring in his step. "It more than covers them, because he's paid me more than I earned. He wants me to purchase a better woodstove than that pile of rusted iron that came with the house when I bought it from him." The tone of his voice changed significantly when he added, "Mr. McDuff is very ill."

"Well, if a new woodstove is his dying wish, perhaps you should do what he says," Emily suggested.

"First I'll see Mr. Thistlethorn," he said firmly. "Then I'll place my order for the stove."

"Mom, can I, um, may I go with Mr. O'Reilly?" Donald asked, correcting himself.

"If he says it's okay," I said.

"Swell," he remarked.

"Button your vest and put your sweater back on," I had to add.

Darby was happy to have Donald's company and we ladies departed.

<hr>

Emily and I strolled along holding hands. For the first part of the way Emma was silent. Sometimes the depth of her daydreaming or reminiscing engendered in her a certain vagueness of manner, but her inattention seldom lasted long, and never gave offense, because she possessed so much kindness. Chatting once again, she shared one of her meditations aloud. "God is able to do exceedingly abundantly more than we ever ask or think."

"Yes," I said, "by the hand of Providence."

Chapter Twenty

November Days

Where there's a will, there's a way.
English proverb

Blackberry Inn was closed for the season. That weekend Michael and I bought the children shoes in Bridgeton and I purchased some odds and ends to hide away for Christmas. I also found the cord and satin Emma needed to finish Elspeth's muff.

On Sunday afternoon we all admired Darby's work on his house. The whitewash did indeed brighten the inside, but the peeling clapboard outside would have to wait until spring. He had, however, managed to paint the front door a cranberry red, which I always thought made a white house look inviting. He explained to Michael how he had removed the old woodstove piece by piece. We stood in front of its empty space imagining the new one in its place. The floors were sanded, stained, and waxed. "Is this oak?" Michael asked.

"Yes," Darby said, "I hand rubbed it. Beautiful, isn't it?" He admired his handiwork.

Emma said. "As handsome as a fine piece of furniture."

"What's this?" I asked, looking at something soaking in the kitchen sink.

"I need to wash those. I had to take the curtains down to paint," Darby said.

Thinking of bat dust, I said, "Agitate them gently but give them a double wash and triple rinse. Then let them drip dry rather than wring them. Better let me do any mending." If he handwashed curtains like he washed dishes, there would be nothing left to them.

"Oh, would you?"

"These red and white curtains will go nicely with your front door," Emma said. "Is red Elspeth's favorite color?"

"She likes red," he said. He turned to me and said, "I know how busy you are. Are you sure you want to mend the curtains?"

"Mrs. Bingham told me today that Miss Crabtree will be returning during the week. The children will start back with her next Monday." I told him. This was the first my children had heard of it.

"So you won't be the teacher anymore?" asked Emily.

"I'll still be *your* teacher, darling," I said.

***

Darby continued the tour outside. Potatoes had self-seeded in the old garden plot, he told us. He had dug them up when he was tackling the high weeds and grass and had placed them in the root cellar that was separate from the house. He said it felt good to have something put by. I saw that he had made progress on a woodpile, too. But he didn't think it right to touch Mr. McDuff's apple orchard because at the time he didn't own it.

"It's a pity so many apples went to spoil," said Michael, "but I'm sure you have big plans for next year's harvest."

"Yeah, I do," he said and looked as if he were raring to go right there and then.

"Mom, Dad, look at this," Donald called to us. He was standing atop a tire swing with Emily watching him sail.

"I knew you'd find it," Darby called out, as he started walking through the high grass and down the hillside to an oak tree. "I put that up so that you and Emily will want to visit me."

"Hot dog!" Donald said, using a new expression he must have picked up somewhere.

———

On Monday I displayed a new painting for my class. Miss Mason's students were given a new picture twice a month, but because I would only have my students a short time, I chose new paintings weekly. "A Fisherman," by the Swedish-born artist Anders Zorn was our next picture. It depicts a man and woman standing next to a lamppost, resting their elbows on the stone wall of the bridge, watching the river run. We see only the backs of the couple. The fisherman's boots are folded down to his knees. The young woman wears a long dress, tight in the waist and full in the skirt. I gave the children some tidbits about the artist, starting with the fact that when Mr. Zorn was a boy, he carved animals in wood, and afterwards colored them with fruit juice. As he matured, so did his desire to paint the sea. I told the children, "It is difficult to paint water, especially waves, which are always in motion. It takes a quick eye and hand to transfer the details of a wave to canvas." They were suitably impressed.

We began our history chapter on William Brewster and the Separatists. I was glad to have reached the pilgrims before the Thanksgiving holiday. While the children drew and put captions to their history drawings, I played our record of Frederic Chopin's piano music again. Hearing the same record played over and over was pleasing to them. They were becoming familiar with a classical repertoire they would be able to recognize in future and maybe even grow to love.

Knowing I would be reading about Indians and Indian corn, I had planned to bake some cornbread for the children in Blackberry

Inn's old cooking fireplace. I had lit a fire before breakfast. Emily picked some leaves still clinging to a maple tree for me. The children watched me line two Dutch ovens with the yellow leaves and spoon the cornmeal batter on top. "The leaves keep the cornbread from sticking to the pot," I said. I raked the glowing embers into a small pile and slid the Dutch ovens over them, surrounding them with embers, too. "This is how cornbread was made in colonial days," I explained.

While the cornbread was baking on the hearth, the children sat cross-legged on the sitting room rug as they had done before. It was the first time I had paid any attention to Emma's braided rug, or taken a close look at it. It had to have been made with the wool scraps she collected in her ragbag. I liked how she had braided the rustic colors together. The children listened while I read from my science book the chapter about air. It explained why ice is placed near the top of an icebox and why warm air rises up a chimney. The examples given were of everyday ordinary things. Examples were also of the extraordinary kind, such as the history of air ships and the Wright brothers. I was looking forward to hearing the children narrate what I would read later in the week about the lift of an airplane wing, the work of the propeller, and the airplanes of the Great War, because I knew Donald and the other boys would be especially interested.

Emma's wrought-iron Dutch ovens were so heavy that I had difficulty maneuvering them. On my knees before the fire, I was able to turn the cornbread onto our widest wooden boards. I didn't want to risk cracking any platters. Those colonial housewives must have had arms and backs as strong as oxen. I let the children take turns peeling away the leaves by their stems. The leaves left a pretty pattern on the bread that was clear for all to see. Lard and our fresh eggs made the bread moist and delicious, but it still crumbled to the floor with every bite. Everyone enjoyed a thick piece before heading home. Little Lydia was sitting with Emily and Sarah. I was happy to see Emily had made a friend of her. The slice of cornbread Emily passed to Lydia was extra thick.

Emily, too, thought to bring her grandmother in for some cornbread. "Mmm, it has a roasted flavor. I've never tasted cornbread as good as this," Emma said to the children with a grin. The children adored her. She magnanimously ignored the fact that her braided rug was covered with yellow crumbs. Donald later gave it a good going over with the carpet sweeper, but in the end I decided it should have a proper beating over the fence. "This is another colonial task that

requires a strong back," I told him as we beat the rug together. Beating a rug was my least likable chore, but it was such a fine rug and I felt good about preserving it for Emma's sake.

～～

One afternoon I had some help in making my autumn specialty—shepherd's pie with a creamy whipped-potato topping. Emily stood on a stepping stool at the sink, scrubbing potatoes clean for me, while Darby and Donald peeled them at the table. I was adding the right spice to the beans and chopped meat I had been simmering. "These potatoes of yours, Darby, are so nice and fresh. They're as crisp and juicy as apples," I said. He felt good about bringing us some for our supper.

"That's why they're called *pomme de terre*, Mom," said Donald. "Mademoiselle Geraldine says they're apples of the earth."

"Whoever made up the French word for potato had good sense," I told him.

～～

That same day Mr. Fortesque was in Appleton to oversee his factory, and that afternoon his car pulled into the drive before Michael's did.

Emily could see out the window over the sink, and announced, "Mr. Fortesque's here." Then we heard his car door slam.

Darby stood up and looked over Emily's shoulder to get a look out the window, too, and said, "Here comes himself. I'm eager to hear news." But he went back to peeling.

A moment later Emma emerged from her bedroom and entered the kitchen proudly. She said, "Darby, it's done. What do you think?" Her hands were tucked into a large rabbit fur muff. It was the warmest, fluffiest muff I had ever seen. The multicolored fur would match a coat and shoes of any shade.

"I, I, t'ink it's beautiful," Darby said.

"Good. You can try it on and feel the satin inside after your hands are washed," she said.

"Go ahead, Darby," I said. He left the room and Emily and I got a closer look without touching it.

"You made that?" Emily asked, with amazement. She was impressed.

"Go ahead, wash your hands, too," I said to Emily. "Perhaps Grandma will also let you try it on," Then I remembered Mr. Fortesque and stepped into the sitting room. I found him waiting on the sofa with his coat on. His back was bent, his elbows resting on his knees. He held his hat in both hands. There he sat, motionless, staring into his hat as if it were ten feet deep. Mr. Fortesque had composure but I could tell something was amiss. He saw me enter and rose politely. I greeted him. "Good afternoon Mr. Fortesque. May I take your coat and hat?"

"Oh, yes, thank you," he said. "Good afternoon, my dear." I stood close beside him while he handed me his things. He looked me in the eyes and said slowly, "Would you please tell Darby I'd like to have a word?" It was the first time I had seen his eyes up close. They were neither blue nor green, but something in between.

"Yes, of course," I said. "Coffee?"

"No, thank you."

Michael arrived and was hanging up his own hat and coat by the time Darby and I entered the sitting room. One look at Mr. Fortesque's uneasy expression, and fear dropped like a heavy stone into the well of Darby's heart, swelling the water to his eyes. I heard him mumble, "Say it isn't so." Then in a louder but less than steady voice, he told Mr. Fortesque, "I'd like my friends to hear."

"That's fine." Being a man of compassion, Mr. Fortesque placed a firm hand on Darby's back while Darby blew his nose on a handkerchief.

Michael diplomatically took charge. "Shall we go into the library?" he said, leading the way. We followed. "Do sit down," Michael said. Mr. Fortesque sat across from Darby at the library table. Michael closed the door behind us.

Mr. Fortesque began. "I might have found your wife, but I might not have." Darby sat on the edge of his chair and inclined his head in reply, waiting to hear more.

Mr. Fortesque took in a deep breath, a sort of backward sigh, and began again. "I'm head of the committees for three soup kitchens. The kitchens are run by churches in and around Bridgeton. I explained to the workers in charge who it was that I was looking for, but told them little, impressing upon them the importance of being discreet. As soon as I was told about one young mother and son, I posted a notice that we needed some kitchen help. The day this mother responded, we discovered her name was Elspeth and her son, Andrew, so we gave her the job."

The veins in Darby's neck looked tense. He sat as still as a cat in front of a mouse hole and would not interrupt the flow of Mr. Fortesque's story.

"We offered her a warm place to live below the kitchen, daily food, and a small payment, in return for work," Mr. Fortesque continued. "The ladies in the kitchen eventually won her confidence and were told that she had no husband, nor any living relatives in America. And I'm hesitant to add, but perhaps you should know, that I've been told this Elspeth is a hard and bitter woman."

Darby spoke finally. "What do you mean, 'this Elspeth'?"

"Her name is Elspeth Keegan."

Leaning back in his chair Darby gave out a short hearty laugh. "Ha, she's using her father's name. Keegan means fiery. That's herself. She must be flaming mad at me. T'anks, Mr. Fortesque. T'anks, for finding me wife. Have you seen her?"

Mr. Fortesque's wilted countenance changed into a victorious one. He had found the right woman. His search was over. "Aye, and the bairn," he said. "But we've all been cautious not to mention *you*, especially since supposedly you don't exist. Therefore we need to come up with another plan, don't we? We need a plan to get you together. How about half-past-seven in the sitting room? This is a three pipe problem, I think."

Darby shook Mr. Fortesque's right hand with both of his. He breathed out more thank-you's and left the room.

As I rose to leave, too, I heard Michael tell Mr. Fortesque, "A 'three pipe problem' sounds like something Sherlock Holmes would say."

"Precisely," Mr. Fortesque said with a lifted eyebrow. "It was Conan Doyle's 'Red-Headed League' that gave me the idea to advertise a position wanted, to unsuspectingly keep Mrs. O'Reilly close by."

His previous years as an advertising man made Michael's handshake of approval genuine. "Capital piece of work," he said.

"Don't mention it, my good man," Mr. Fortesque replied, with a triumphant pat of his moustache with his thick fingers, which half hid a smile that gave away just how very pleased he was with himself. "Don't mention it."

Chapter Twenty-one

An Important Meeting

To make a happy
fireside clime
For bairns and wife,
Is the true pathos an'
sublime
Of human life.

Robert Burns

On the children's outing to Mr. and Mrs. Percival's house I was blessed to have Emma's company again. Her rapport with my charges gave them happy faces because she enjoyed them so thoroughly. She had a way of sympathizing with even any subtle sense of wonder a child might display. She had probably told each child at one time or another that he or she was "so cute." Even the boys who approached her height didn't mind. The children set out with their readers under their arms and an apple in their mouths. It was a little longer walk to the Percivals than to our other outings, and well before we arrived apple cores had been tossed into woods and fingers licked. Mittens that were stuffed into coat pockets were slipped on at my command. The air smelled of impending snow.

I came prepared with questions to help Mr. Percival with his demonstration of making a broom out of broomcorn. It proved to be a wise preparation. Even though he was keen, he was shy with an audience and he mumbled. I was able to interpret for the children without offending him. We were informed that the old log cabin, which was just big enough for us all to stand inside, had been built by one of Mr. Percival's ancestors, with *his bare hands*. The cabin served as a work shed for Mr. Percival. We stood watching him as he made his broom with admirable precision. He wove the corn sheaves with jute, using a heavy double-pointed needle that had its hole midway down its length. "The hole is there so that he can turn it any way he pleases as he binds the corn," I told the children. The boys liked the wooden contraption that held the broom in place and allowed Mr. Percival to bind the sheaves tightly. The sharp sickle-shaped corn cutter put a straight edge on the bottom of the broom and the job was finished. I gave my compliments to Mr. Percival and, picking out a large broom, asked him to set it aside for me. "For a Christmas present," I told him. I was thinking of Bob and Dora. He responded happily, saying, "Your man says I should sell my brooms at the Apple Butter Festival next year."

"You have my vote," I said.

Mrs. Percival was less daunted than her husband when surrounded by children. She had ready for us three batches of goat's milk soap in three different stages of preparation. Although she had inherited hillbilly grammar, she was cheery and personable in her talk, and I was appreciative. In closing, she placed into the hand of each child a tiny piece of smooth soap to take home to his or her mother. It was the best advertising for her wares that she could ever hope for, but I don't think this was her purpose.

I shook hands with my students as we made our farewells. This was our last outing, and our last day of school together. Sarah gave me a hug. "I'm going to miss them," I told Emma, as I watched my curls and cowlicks walk away. But liberty regained felt good, too.

"Them kids is a nice bunch. Cuppa tea?" Mrs. Percival said, eager for female conversation. "I make it nice'n strong."

"We'd love a cup, Phoebe," said Emma, "but we're off to Bridgeton as soon as we get home."

"Sounds important," Mrs. Percival said. Emma only smiled. She would not confide further and risk having the news travel through Appleton's vigorous grapevine.

Mrs. Percival wasn't ready to let us go. She said to me, "So, you're living in Emma's house?" Her words were jarring to me. I had to curb my agitation. To the children, she said, "How do yous like it here?"

"It's swell!" Donald exclaimed. I said nothing. I could tell Emma's eyes were upon me, but I wouldn't meet them.

"Have you heard that the outsider is back? O'Reilly, his name is."

It was imprudent of me to add to this, but I felt compelled to credit him. "He's considered to be a hard worker."

"Strange his family ain't here."

My sweetie Emily said, "The little boy's lost. Mr. Fortesque's looking for him. We're going to..."

Before she uttered another word I said, "Children, why not try to catch up with Seth and Sarah. They can't be far ahead."

"Come on, Emily, let's go." Donald said, inadvertently coming to my rescue.

"We'll meet up with you at their house," I called after them. Fingering some coins in my purse, I asked Mrs. Percival, "How much for two bars of your creamy soap?"

This changed her line of thinking, and her mood also lifted when she cut me the bars. She said, "Your brother keeps your parents' place real nice. He married a city girl, didn't he? Some say she's prissy. Won't getter hands dirty. It's a shame 'bout your folks. Thems were nice people."

I wanted next to credit my sister-in-law, but bit my tongue. I didn't know where to begin and was getting too agitated anyway to speak with enough civility on the subject. I thanked her again for being our hostess and Emma chimed in at last, repeating her earlier statement. "We must be off."

Yet Mrs. Percival was only warming up. "You'll never guess what I seen pinned to Penelope Bingham's clothesline when I was there last w..."

Emma had pluck. "Phoebe, keep it to yourself. We don't want to hear it," she insisted in the manner of an older sister. She put a hand on my shoulder to nudge me to start walking. So I did. But I twisted around at a safe distance and said to Mrs. Percival as she stood watching us go, "I can't wait to use my new soap. Good-bye."

She gave me a sincere yellow-toothed grin and said, "Come again."

~~~

Emma and I walked toward town. "You might have warned me," I said.

"I'm sorry," she responded.

"I thought we'd never get out of there," I said.

"Nor did I—safely, that is," Emma said. "Phoebe's propensity for gossip is phenomenal. I've learned the hard way that she can keep nothing to herself. The funny thing is that she's not offended when I tell her plainly to stop."

Once in town we stepped into the general store. I purchased the red yarn I had had my eye on and filled my basket with groceries. Emma enjoyed picking out some embroidery floss. Upon leaving the store we spotted Michael. He had guessed we would be in town. As we drove up to the side of the Bingham's house to pick up the children, I couldn't help noticing Penelope's clothesline. A pulley was attached to the trunk of a tall tree. The other pulley was attached somewhere near her kitchen door, no doubt. Thus the long line of wash hung quite visibly up above the fence. It was pinned in an orderly manner in groups as it was washed: darks, colors, and whites, with nothing curiously strange about it. "Oh, the power of gossip. It's hard to resist," I mused.

Mr. Fortesque was out back when we returned to Blackberry Inn. He had just come from one of his walks. Very soon the cars were packed with Mr. Fortesque's welcome committee. He and Emma were in one car. Michael, Darby, the children, and one custom-made muff, were in the other. Michael was glad that I was staying behind to rest and so was I. Life had been full of such excitement in Appleton as I never thought possible, and I was looking forward to a quiet evening to myself.

Once I was alone I sat down at an empty kitchen table. The sink was polished and shiny. Not a dish stood on the draining board, not a crumb on the floor, and I meant to keep it that way. Therefore an early supper was simplicity itself. I sliced a thick piece of Emma's wheat bread and spread butter and blackberry jam to excess. Hearing the faint hoot of an owl that had apparently just awakened made me think of new and wise beginnings. Darby had been filled with anticipation when he waved good-bye. He was experiencing a new

beginning, and so were we, with our new life in Appleton and a new baby on the way. I buttered another slice of bread and enjoyed the tranquility of the moment. What were those lines from the poem "Out to Old Aunt Mary's" I had read to the children that morning? Something, something, *with sunshine spread as thick as butter on country bread...*

I was feeling too lazy to make myself a pot of tea, but took some apple pie and a glass of milk into the sitting room. Since no one was watching, I put my legs up on the sofa. It was my habit to reflect during moments of solitude. I prayed that the plan of getting Darby and Elspeth together would go well. He would be hiding in the storage room during the hustle and bustle of kitchen cleanup. Elspeth would be told to bring something into that room. Meanwhile Donald and Emily would entertain Andrew by blowing soap bubbles. In the privacy of the storeroom the couple could come to an understanding. It was our hope that they would be reunited by mutual forgiveness.

After washing my few dishes, I thought, "What do I do?" A bath, definitely, but first I felt the need to read Emma's bookmarked poem again. My recent visit to the Percivals had left me longing for moral support. Since I was by myself with no one to spy on me, I took the poetry book off the shelf, sat in the library, and read it in uninterrupted silence. If this were my house, what would I change to make it all my own? I stopped midway upstairs to scan the foyer, entrance hall, and sitting room below. Then I climbed the rest of the stairs, stood on the landing, and looked around me. "Nothing," I thought. "I would change nothing." I liked it just as it was. A home isn't a house, anyway. A home is a life shared with family, friends, and welcomed strangers—a place to work, rest, worship, play, and grow, a place to laugh and mourn in safety. It's a place where memories are made.

Soaking in a hot tub, I felt at peace. My bath, an early dark sky, and the ambient stillness of the large house put me in repose. It was only six o'clock. Michael and the gang wouldn't return until half-past eight, and Blackberry Inn was ready for them. A bedroom for Darby and Elspeth had been freshened with a lavender sachet. Emma had rolled out the trundle bed for Andrew and had given it a satin-edged blanket. The rocking horse was set up in the living room, the high chair in the dining room. In my robe I sank into an easy chair. With my knitting basket beside me, I reached for a skein of my new red yarn. First I wound it into a ball. Then I cast on stitches for my first mitten and began "knit two, purl two" ribbing for the cuff. My blue dress had been laid out on the bed. I wanted to look presentable for their arrival.

The doorknocker startled me. It made the sound of a bass drum as it echoed up the long staircase. I looked up at the clock in blank astonishment. It read ten minutes to seven. I must have dozed. My knitting was in a tangle at my feet. Who could it be? In the children's room I peeked through the curtains and saw the outline of Bob's truck in the moonlight. I ran my fingers through my damp hair, tied my robe tighter, and trotted down the cold stairs barefooted, thinking, "No more excitement, please."

"Hi, Sis. Are you feeling all right?"

"Yes, and you? I took a bath, that's all. Come in, Dora, come in. Make yourselves at home." We were all standing in the dark, so I turned on a light in the sitting room. "Come in and sit down," I said. Bob was carrying Jonathan, who was half asleep. He was bundled up in a blanket with his face half covered by an oversized hat, knit in three shades of brown. The hat had ear flaps and was tied under his chubby chin. "He's so cute when he's sleepy," I said. "Is this his new hat?"

Dora said, "Yes. I just finished it. Do you like it? We're only staying a short while, Carol."

"Then we need to go home and hit the hay," said Bob, trying to shake off a yawn. But it was too large a yawn to hide.

"Excuse me while I go up and dress. It's chilly in here. Would you put another log on, Bob? Turn on another light, too, if you like, Dora."

"Sis, we came to pray with you for Darby, for the reconciliation of his family."

"Oh, I see. Good idea," I said, "where two or more are gathered. I'll only be a minute." I shivered from the chill as I climbed the stairs.

Chapter Twenty-two

Chamomile Tea in the Moonlight

What soap is to the body, tears are to the soul.

Jewish proverb

"Where are they?" I sat in the sitting room, keeping an eye on the door, waiting for them. I could not concentrate on my book. At any moment I expected to hear a car. It was when I finally got up to get my knitting to busy my hands that I heard a car pull in. It was Mr. Fortesque, Emma, and the children. Emma immediately started the kettle boiling to make a pot of chamomile tea, at the same time giving me the news. "They're coming, dear. Isn't it wonderful?"

"They've called a truce," Mr. Fortesque smiled.

"A reason to rejoice," I said.

"Mommy, you should see Andrew. He's a funny little boy," Emily said.

Donald added, "Who doesn't like soap bubbles."

"Oh, what did you do with him, then?" I asked.

Emily explained. "We showed him how to make fists and count one potato, two potato, three potato, four."

Donald said, "He liked that. We did it over and over. I never knew a kid that found it so funny."

"You taught him something new. Very good, children." I asked them to tell me about what they had observed at the soup kitchen. With many "and thens" they described to me all that they had seen and all that had taken place. By the time they had finished, Emma had her steeping teapots on their trays. "Well, it has been a full day. Bedtime," I announced.

～～

We all went upstairs. Mr. Fortesque carried one tray of tea into his room and Emma carried the other tray into the room of the happy couple. Having started the children on their bedtime routine, I went back downstairs to meet Michael at the front door.

"You're here!" I exclaimed as Elspeth entered. "Welcome." Michael introduced us. "And this is Andrew?" I asked, stooping by his side. I wasn't expecting to feel such affection for them. The feeling came upon me suddenly. At long last they were where they ought to be—with Darby. "Welcome, welcome," I said again. Elspeth gave me a strained smile. The large muff dangled on her wrist by its cord. In the dim light I saw that her face was fair and freckled, her blue eyes framed in a whisper of lashes, her dark hair braided down her back. She was so diminutive and wide-eyed that she resembled a lost elf. I had a hard time imagining her to be fiery. Leaning up against his mother was Andrew. He resembled his father, but I couldn't exactly say how. With one hand he sucked his thumb, and with the other he stroked his mother's muff as if it were a stuffed Teddy. I spoke to

Elspeth. "You must be tired from your journey. Would you like me to show you up to your room?"

"Yes, I'd like that," she said. "It's been quite a day, thank you." She looked up at the ceiling and all around her as we walked through the sitting room. Blackberry Inn seemed particularly dark and cavernous that night and the old staircase seemed to creak more loudly than usual. Andrew clung to his mother as we climbed slowly up the stairs.

"Will he let me carry him up?" Darby asked his wife. She gave him an uncertain yes. But Darby showed wisdom by holding Andrew so that he faced his mother. Michael followed us up with the bags. I informed the couple that Mrs. Cook had just put a pot of her home-made brew of restful tea in their room, and that I was looking forward to seeing them again in the morning.

They were not at all talkative, weary of words, perhaps. "Good night," they both said, without looking at me. Like newlyweds, they couldn't keep their eyes off each other.

"Phew, that's done," Michael said, when we were alone together in our bedroom, What a full day it had been for him.

"Why wasn't this scheme scheduled for Saturday, rather than at the end of a full day of work?" I asked in a critical tone.

"Mr. Fortesque needs to be heading back early in the morning. He's traveling out of state again." Michael got into bed and laid his head on his pillow. He recalled the evening's events. "I had my doubts when I heard the way Elspeth was carrying on at first. I felt sure she wasn't going to come back with us. She was so angry with Darby that she became hysterical, Carol. She cried and scolded and then cried some more."

"That comes from deep hurt," I said. "The heaviest thing to carry is a grudge. She probably felt Darby had abandoned them, although it was *she* who couldn't face *him*. Also 'make-do-and-mend' is one thing. Going around with a begging bowl in her hand is quite another. I'm guessing she took care of her mother as she was dying, too. All those things must've been hard."

"Yes, well, I would have felt more sympathy if I had considered those things. But not being as insightful as you..." He paused and kissed my hand. "All I could think of was that the kitchen clean-up was so noisy that no one was paying any attention. And that the storeroom door was thick enough to muffle her high-pitched sobs. Then I spotted his peace offering and realized that Darby had forgotten to take it."

"The muff?"

"Yes, the muff. I wasn't sure whether it would be best to knock on the door or not. But I did. Darby opened it just wide enough for me to pass it to him."

"I would've liked to have seen her face after she unwrapped it," I said.

"It was very quiet after that; not a sound came from either of them. So I went over to the children and added my fists to their potato-counting. Ten minutes later we were collecting Elspeth's meager belongings and were off. Phew," he said again, turning on his side, pulling the covers over his ears, and closing his eyes.

"I'm so happy they're together. Thanks, Michael." I moved the blanket from his ear and kissed it. "Sleep tight," I said softly. Within minutes my physically and emotionally worn man was fast asleep.

Unlike Michael, I lay awake with the moon shining on my face. Getting out of bed to close the gap in the curtains, I realized how hungry I was. Not normally one for nighttime snacks, my stomach was gurgling loud enough to convince me to creep downstairs for a little something.

When I entered the dark kitchen I was not expecting to see the shape of someone sitting in the dark. It was Emma, with a steaming cup of chamomile tea before her. She was dripping honey into it. "What's the matter, dear? You look as though you've seen a ghost. Do sit down. Is the full moon keeping you up?"

"How did you know?"

"It has a way of keeping me up. And it's been an exciting day, hasn't it? Toast?"

"Please."

"Tea?"

"Yes, please." I sat quietly while she served me. She was deftly at ease in the kitchen, even in the dark, and I found it soothing.

"You're showing very nicely now," she said.

"Thank you. I always feel better when I show, and when I can feel the baby moving."

"Me, too," she said as if she was in her childbearing years as well. Emma often forgot her age.

Another ghost appeared silhouetted in the dark doorway of the kitchen. "Pardon me. I hope I'm not intruding." It was Mr. Fortesque, in his smoking jacket and slippers.

Emma smiled, and said apologetically, "Did you smell the toast all the way up the stairs?"

"Aye, and it made me hungry."

"Thick or thinly sliced?"

"Thick dry toast, please."

The three of us sat in the moonlight saying only little. Out of a sense of propriety I stayed until after Mr. Fortesque had bid us a final good night. Later, while I lay under my covers with a much quieter stomach, the thought did cross my mind that the night's meeting had been a previously planned one. Maybe Mr. Fortesque was sneaking downstairs just as he had been sneaking into that alley door. But there was no need to tell Michael anything about my musings. Why strengthen his opinion of my suspicious nature? I fell asleep, guilty of breaking my resolve not to depreciate Mr. F.

Chapter Twenty-three

Snow in the Woods

You can give without loving, but you cannot love without giving.
Amy Carmichael

Over the next weeks I enjoyed having my children all to myself. I began the mornings with close attention to spelling after a poem. Their lapse in spelling was intentional. While Appleton's children were in my charge, I had made it a priority to offer them a wide scope of knowledge during the limited time I had with them. Spelling they would always have as a subject. The opportunity to gain knowledge by narration, however, they would have for only a very short time. Therefore my children also went without spelling for the weeks that I had taught my class. Miss Mason was opposed to evening homework, and I agreed with her so I had not given spelling as homework either. But now they were studying their words twice in one day to dedicate them to memory.

~~~

For Picture Study I displayed "The Farmer's Daughter" by Sir William Quiller Orchardson. The young girl in the painting stands in the doorway of a barn feeding pigeons. Emily could relate to this since she feeds the chickens. She also liked the girl's pink muslin gown, a style of the early part of the nineteenth century.

Longfellow's "Courtship of Miles Standish" fit in well with our study of the Separatists, though Donald was not particularly fond of this long poem. Next we read about the Puritans in the Massachusetts Bay Colony. Among the pages describing how the Puritans lived was a picture showing a woman at a spinning wheel in front of a wide fireplace. I noticed that Emily was embellishing her narration with things she had experienced in her own life. She spoke of Dora at her spinning wheel and of my cornbread cooking at the hearth. If embellishments were against the rules of narrating, I would make an exception for the time being. Emily had made her own associations and I wasn't about to snuff out the flame.

We read about Roger Williams, the Pequot, Narragansett, and Wampanoag Indians, and the Puritan John Eliot. Donald helped fill in the details not supplied by our history book. He told us how Eliot had supervised fourteen settlements where more than a thousand Indian converts could live in peace. They were known as the praying Indians. Our history book and Eliot's biography both told the sad tale of how these praying Indians were scattered and killed by warring Indian tribes during King Philip's War. It was Donald, not I, who commented on the contrast between good and evil during the colonial days.

I decided to take some time for the children to make entries into their science notebooks of the chapters I had read aloud to the class in previous weeks. They entered drawings and a written narration of the history of airships. Using a rainbow of bright colors, Emily drew a balloon in flight. Donald took great pains to copy as accurately as he could three models of airplanes pictured in the book. He did much erasing and was as thoroughly absorbed in the task as if he had found a new hobby. This freed me to sit alongside Emily to help her with what little writing I expected of her.

I thought I might get to know Elspeth better during her stay with us, but she was far more comfortable talking with Emma, and did so every day, while I did lessons with the children. Donald liked giving Andrew a ride in the wheelbarrow in the afternoons. He also showed him how to build with wooden blocks. Yet Andrew was capable of entertaining himself. Next to using up energy on the rocking horse, his favorite activity was wheeling one of Donald's metal steam engines noisily back and forth along the wooden floor. "Mom," Donald shared with me one day, "I hope your baby is a boy."

In the evenings, just before getting to bed, I would work on a mitten. I could finish one mitten in three evenings. Andrew's I did in two. I knit the cuffs nice and snug by using my narrow sock needles for the ribbing, changing to larger needles for the body of the mitten. There is nothing so annoying when building a snowman as a wet mitten sagging at the wrist. I wrote riddles in anticipation of the first day of snow. The year before, at our first snowfall, I had hidden their new mittens in the house, giving the children each a riddle about where to find them. This year I wanted to do the same, and thus make it a tradition. An issue of *Mother's Companion* claimed that anything a mother does with her family for two consecutive years becomes a family tradition.

Just before Thanksgiving the O'Reillys' new woodstove arrived at the general store and was installed that very day, with the help of the owner of the store himself. Elspeth's smile to me was no longer strained, and on that morning she wore the softest countenance. She had been looking forward to being in her own home, especially after seeing it all clean and whitewashed, with curtains looking so crisp and fresh hanging in the windows, and that day had arrived. Emma gave her a housewarming gift. She had devoted some hours embroidering the motto "Home Sweet Home" on punched paper. Its letters were satin-stitched in candy cane colors and accented with red roses. What had Darby said about America that had ended the round table of discussion awhile back? "God bless America, my home sweet home." I imagined Emma's motto reflected such sentiments, as well as those regarding moving into their house. I had my patchwork pillow ready, and I had also picked out a variety of preserves from the cellar, tied them up with fabric and ribbon, and wrapped them with brown paper for careful transport to their house.

Elspeth was touched by our gestures of friendship. Not too proud to accept our gift, she even gave Emma a hug. To befriend someone is the better gift, one Emma had done first this time. I had been touched by what Darby had shared with me in private: "Your family has given us a sense of belonging, the best gift of all. T'anks." That was it. Darby had hit the nail on the head for me. A deeper sense of belonging is what I had been waiting and wishing for.

The O'Reillys wished to spend Thanksgiving Day on their own, and hoped that Bob and Dora would not take offense when they declined their invitation. Dora said, "At what better time could you celebrate your homecoming?"

When we piled into the car on Thanksgiving Day, I realized how much I had been looking forward to spending the holiday at my childhood home. "It has been ages since we've had you over," Dora said, when Emma and I walked into the kitchen and handed her our covered dishes. The kitchen smelled wonderfully of garlic, thyme, and sage.

"It smells just like my mother's cooking in here," I told Dora. "It's making my mouth water." She seemed pleased at this. "Her turkey stuffing was always carefully herbed and full of chopped celery and onion," I added. Although holidays made me miss my parents most, on this visit I was not reserved about sharing remembrances of them, and chatted about them as I hadn't done before. Emma apparently sensed it was safe to add her own fond remembrances of my mother. She liked having the freedom to talk about the friendship she had enjoyed for so many years, and so chatted about whatever came to mind.

As Emily and I were setting the table, Donald announced to us that Mr. Fortesque's car had pulled up. I placed another dish at the table and Bob brought another chair. It would be a tight squeeze.

Bob confided in me. "I wasn't sure he'd come. He's a man Dad would've liked, so I thought to invite him. Months ago Mr. Fortesque arranged to take my surplus for his soup kitchens. The rest of my sales were made with his connections and personal endorsement. I don't think I could've put money by for pasteurization without him. Don't let on like you know, Sis. He was taught to do good deeds with what he calls concealment, and takes it seriously."

"I won't, Bob." I winked.

I did not wash or dry a single dish that entire day. This was because Dora shooed me out of the kitchen after we all finished eating and so I joined the men in the parlor. Donald and Emily sat on the rug and rolled a ball back and forth along the floor to entertain Jonathan. I sank into the cushions of the sofa next to Michael and a wave of comfortable relaxation settled upon me. I was sitting in the same flower-patterned sofa that had been in the parlor for as long as I could remember. Between the parlor curtains tiny snowflakes fell so slowly and gently that they floated on the air. My round stomach and the fullness of the meal kept me anchored. Mid-January my baby would be born, God willing. He might even have the same birthday as Jonathan.

Bob reached down and swung Jonathan onto his lap and asked Emily if she'd like to give his horse, Rhubarb, a carrot. He knew how much she enjoyed this. Donald wanted to swing on the rope in the loft, so together they left for the barn.

"Michael, a word?" Mr. Fortesque entreated. His requests were always given with the natural authoritativeness of someone entrusted with the weight of responsibility early in life, and men were easily inclined to oblige him. Perhaps his responsibilities were heavier than ever. Something tightened his brow.

The two men disappeared into the cold outdoors. In a few weeks the canning factory would be closed for winter. Michael would be out of employment until mid-spring. Mr. Fortesque would be occupied with other business and would not need to be a guest at Blackberry Inn until spring. This, I was told, was the way of things. Michael had been putting money by for the winter and I had saved some of my own scant earnings from teaching. We would do fine with our roots and jars in the cellar. The wash would again become a chore of mine in order for us to preserve our cash until Blackberry Inn reopened in May. I was looking forward to having Michael home to teach the children after the baby was born and to keep the woodstoves fed for us.

The men returned. I could hear their deep voices as they chuckled in the center hall, where they hung up their coats and hats. Yes, they must have gone into the barn, because the children had come in with them. Michael cracked a window when he re-entered the parlor. He was poised to light his pipe but he wouldn't strike his match when he saw that Mr. Fortesque did not light his. Instead, Michael got up and closed the window. Whatever might have been troubling Mr. Fortesque seemed to have disappeared after his walk with Michael. His jolly self had returned. He leaned his head back into a cushioned chair and looked content. "Ho-ho, Donald, my good lad," he said with deep-voiced gaiety. "Get out the checkers. Let's have a game."

Donald stood up to find it and spoke candidly. "Mr. Fortesque, you sound like Santa Claus."

"I am Santa Claus."

Emily overheard, and wasn't going to be fooled. "You can't be the real Santa Claus," she protested.

Mr. Fortesque replied, "Nay, lassie, I have to admit that I'm not. But at the soup kitchens I pretend to be. Every December I get my red costume out of the attic and make believe I'm Father Christmas, or old Saint Nick, if you like. Life has been hard for a lot of people, but it's good to see them smile at Christmastime." During this conversation Emma had walked into the parlor and found a seat next to the piano bench where my quiet brother was sitting. She gave away what she was thinking.

"Your whiskers are certainly whiter, but I'm afraid you'll have to use two or three pillows under your costume this year, Mr. Fortesque."

"Mrs. Cook, are you saying I no longer look the part?"

"I suppose I am," she said. He pretended to be shocked at this, so she soothed him. "But you'll always be Santa at heart," she added. Mr. Fortesque tilted his head back, crossed his arms over his stomach, and let out an even louder belly laugh. His "ho, ho, ho" had such authenticity that it roused us all to laughter. But it spooked poor Jonathan, who wailed in fright. Bob cradled him like a newborn in his efforts to calm him but in less than a minute Dora entered the room to see what was the matter. A second round of laughter broke out when the incident was explained to her.

Chapter Twenty-four

Mr. Right

*Whoso findeth
a wife findeth a
good thing.*
Proverbs 18:22

$\mathcal{I}$t snowed again last night," Michael said, as I awoke. He had just entered the room. "I fed the woodstoves and had breakfast."

"I must have overslept," I said, rubbing the sand from my eyes.

"That's understandable, in your roly-poly condition."

"Yes well, it's time I *rolled* out of bed. More snow, did you say?"

"A few inches. The sun's out, so it might start melting by the afternoon. In another two days you won't have to worry about me driving in it. Anyway, Mr. Fortesque is waiting downstairs. I must dash."

"Wait, what if it doesn't melt and Mr. Fortesque is stuck here?" I was thinking aloud.

"I don't think he'd mind, do you?"

~~~

I entered the children's room. "Up and at 'em," I said. December's darker mornings were keeping them in bed longer. "Emily, it's your turn to open the next window on our Advent calendar isn't it?" Their anticipation of our new morning ritual got them both moving. I think I was wise to hang the calendar in the kitchen.

~~~

My goal was to progress as far into our studies as I could before Christmas and before the baby arrived. Our Picture Study for the advent season was Sandro Botticelli's "Madonna and Child." Mary's face is painted in idyllic serenity. The infant Jesus sweetly clings to her. The fabric of her garments is edged in delicately embroidered gold. Mr. Chesterton says that the "bright gold in the picture is a peculiarity of Botticelli's work, and is due to his early training as a goldsmith."

I chose a new composer. Christmas music was being played on the radio, and hearing Franz Schubert's "Ave Maria" the evening before had given me the idea. The piece I had heard was such a beautiful blend of violin, cello, and piano.

Since we were finished with *Black Beauty*, I had collected some poems and stories pertaining to Christmas. I had read Leo Tolstoy's "Story of Martin the Cobbler" from *My Book House* the last two evenings.

~~~

We were up to William Penn and the settlement of Pennsylvania in our history and had finished our study of the solar system in our science book. We were embarking upon a study of the human eye, which included a biographical sketch of Louis Braille, and the human ear, with a look into the life of Alexander Graham Bell. This suggested to me the idea of further reading about the life of scientists and inventors for the following year's study. The idea was attractive to me, but I tucked it away in order to focus on the needs of the present. Emma was having her annual Christmas party for her Sunday school students and their parents. She had also invited a circle of friends. It would be in just two days and I sought to help her by making the fruit cakes ahead of time. The children wanted to put up a Christmas tree in time for it, and had already rummaged in the attic with Emma to find the ornaments.

<center>~~~</center>

It stayed sunny all day and the snow did indeed melt that afternoon, leaving a white covering only in the woods and in the shade under bushes. Emma decided to call on the Goslin sisters. During her visit she would put in her order for a Christmas goose. Although it would be more convenient, she would not dare bring up the subject of commerce and give them her order on a Sunday when she normally saw them. At her departure I stood at the open door, breathing in the cold fresh air. "Don't be long," I told her, like a doting mother.

"I never overdo my stay," she called back to me.

I called back, "That's not what I meant. I meant it might snow some more."

She waved me her assurance while she kept up a brisk pace. There was lightness in her step that told me she was glad to escape to the outdoors again. Before closing the door, I watched some house sparrows flock to a blackberry bush, pecking at its dried berries for seed. The brown females squeaked and griped. The males were dandies that didn't think quarreling worth the bother. Their pinkish plumage stood out against the melting snow. I scanned the trees for my cardinals but found them nowhere.

<center>~~~</center>

Supper was salmon croquettes flavored with dried celery leaves and minced onion. I mixed the salmon with boiled potato, breadcrumbs, and finely grated carrot. The recipe did not call for carrot but I liked how its orange color enhanced the pink presentation of the salmon, which otherwise is lost when using potato and breadcrumbs only. I panfried two days' worth. I was afraid the children would have lost their taste for fish since I had started force-feeding them spoonfuls of cod liver oil—their winter substitute for a daily dose of sunshine. I forced myself to be an example and take it, too, for the sake of the baby. A subsequent spoonful of honey to cleanse the palate was only a small enticement. Cod liver oil tastes horrible, no two ways about it.

At supper Mr. Fortesque wiped his mouth with one of Emma's generously-sized napkins and said, "I can't get croquettes at Waldo's Fish and Poultry. He doesn't make them anymore. Yours are by far more tasty anyway, Carol. I shall miss your cooking more than you can know."

"And we shall miss you," I said. He wasn't expecting this, nor was I, for that matter. It just came out. For a minute he uncharacteristically averted his eyes, keeping them focused on the napkin he was folding.

"Please, allow me to do the washing up," he said, when he looked up again. "And call me Ian."

"If you'd like, Ian," I answered affectionately. Emma started clearing the dishes. Then Michael called all his family to him to tell us to meet him upstairs because he wanted to read us something special for the Advent season. We gathered in the bedroom and made ourselves comfortable. Emma and Ian were downstairs in the kitchen together doing the dishes.

<hr />

Michael read to us part of Edwin Markham's well-known poem, "How the Great Guest Came." Donald commented that it was much like "The Story of Martin the Cobbler."

"Then you should be good at telling me the moral of the story," said his dad.

Donald gave the answer: "Do unto others what you would have others do unto you."

"Yes," Michael said, "but there's more to it." When I had read "Martin the Cobbler" to them I had chosen to let the story speak for itself, but was now curious to know what the children had thought of this part of the poem.

Donald tried again. "Welcome strangers?"

Michael was satisfied. "Well done, Donald."

Emily spoke up, "We had three strangers at our house, too." We knew she was referring to the O'Reilly family. My eyes met Michael's, and he could see how pleased I was at Emily's association. She knew these three had been given a special welcome.

"Yes we did, didn't we?" Michael said. "And you showed Christian kindness to them. You too, Donald."

Then their dad revealed a deeper meaning of the story. "Christ told the disciples that whatever they did for His brethren they were doing for Him."

~——~

Later that evening I asked Michael, "How about a milky drink? I have a craving for one. And I can't find my mending basket."

"Carol, do you have to go downstairs now?" he said to me. "I don't wish you to be under any misapprehension."

"Misapprehension? What about?"

"About Emma and Mr. Fortesque, er, Ian. There's something I need to tell you when you come back upstairs."

"Okay." I said. I walked slowly down the stairs, hoping to catch a bird's-eye view of the sitting room to see if my mending basket was left there, but found instead Emma and Ian sitting side by side on the sofa. The candles in their scones were lit as well as those resting on the fireplace mantle, which made the room look enchanting. I instantly turned around and retraced my steps. Michael was waiting for me on the landing. "I'm very interested to hear what you have to say, Michael," I snapped, and in my current state of roundness, plopped heavily into my easy chair, expecting an answer forthwith.

Michael was taking strides back and forth across the room, deciding where to begin. "Please, do stop pacing, darling," I said in my impatience.

He gave me the long and short of it—the short of it first. "On Thanksgiving Day, Mr. F., er, Ian, told me that since I was in the position of "man of the house," he was asking my permission to court Emma. He wants to do things properly this time."

"Properly?"

"He's going to try for an engagement again but this time he wants to give Emma a proper courtship. He thinks that the reasons Emma turned him down in the past may have something to do with her living alone here, and the fear of marrying a man who will "kick the bucket" on her again. She has already experienced the heartbreak of out-living three husbands. Therefore he decided to increase the investment in his physique."

"Oh, really?" I said, covering my mouth to smother a giggle.

"For his health," he quickly added, trying to maintain seriousness. But my laughter was contagious and he broke out in one of his grand sonorous chuckles.

"I *thought* he'd been looking trim. But he's younger than Emma," I brought to light.

"Not much, not enough to matter."

"How much?" I couldn't resist asking.

"Four years I think. Anyway, the editor of *Liberty Magazine* also has another magazine called *Physical Culture*. He said Bernarr Macfadden puts out a wealth of information about how to live a healthy life. When Ian was out of state, he was in Danville, New York, at one of Macfadden's health resorts. They teach a regimen of eating less, eating nutritionally, and exercising. By walking and boosting his nutritional intake, he has been feeling better already."

"Michael, you sound like you've been reading the magazine yourself."

"I'm trying to remember his exact words. Apparently this is why he's given up coffee and his pipe. Anyway, there's more." He started pacing again and continued. "His long-range goals meant revamping his leisure, thus he had less time to spend in Appleton. He urged me to be forthright with him, to tell him anything that may concern me about his becoming Emma's suitor. So I took the chance and stuck my neck out. I asked him about the alley door."

"You did? What did he say?"

Michael sat down in his easy chair. "Well, it amazed me that he took it so calmly."

"That's a relief."

"Because he's so well known in Bridgeton he was trying to avoid talk. How did he put it? Oh, yes. He said there's gossip *every twelve feet* along Main Street. So, since his nutritionist lived on Main Street, he had his consultations with her discreetly, using her alley door. If I'd kept my concern to myself, he would have thought less of me, he said.

"This explains everything," I said.

"Yes, it..." Before he could finish his sentence, there was a knock on our bedroom door. Michael got up and opened it as if he were in a business office. It was Ian. "I've peeked in on the children to say good-bye and Merry Christmas. These little gifts are for them. Would you put them in their stockings for me? I'm leaving in the morning. I wanted to wish you a Merry Christmas, too, as I won't be able to stay for Emma's party."

"You'll be needed as 'soup-kitchen-Santa,' won't you?" I asked, smiling.

"Yes," he said, still sounding serious. "I pray all goes well with the bairn."

"Thank you," I nodded. "Will we not see you all winter?" Distracted and in an unusual frame of mind, he did not answer.

Instead he addressed Michael. "Did you ask her?"

"Not yet. Please, come in Ian. You may as well ask her yourself. Take my chair, please," Michael waved his arm wide, gesturing for his boss and friend to become unglued from the doorway.

Mr. Fortesque stepped further into the room and sank down into the cushion of Michael's easy chair, but leaned forward with his elbows on his knees and his hands clasped. "I wanted to know, Carol, how you feel about my courting Mrs. Cook."

"Did she agree to it?" I was intensely curious.

A grin broke through his handlebar moustache and met his side-burns. "Aye." This one word was full of effervescent joy, a joy that sparkled in his blue-green eyes and lit up his whole face. "And she's asked me to call her Emma."

"Has she? Well, we're very fond of you, Ian. You have our bless-ing." I felt like the queen mother on her throne. "You must love her very much if you've been working at becoming the man you imagine to be worthy of her."

"I'll never be worthy of her. I hate having to leave her. It will be my longest winter. What a struggle it's been to keep from proposing again. But I realize now that it's important for a lady to be given a courtship first. For three years I've felt it my business to look after Mrs. Cook." He cleared his throat and corrected himself, "*Emma*. I want to make her happy and keep her from harm. It's what I want to do with the rest of my life." Then he stood up and started speaking a language more comfortable for him. He turned to Michael and said, in a more businesslike tone, "I plan to delegate some of my responsibility, forgo one venture and liquidate another, in order to be more available come spring. I'm also investing in a variety of bargain basement stocks at a dollar a share."

"You're buying?" Michael didn't hide his astonishment.

Our wise friend proceeded to give Michael a brief lesson in economy. "I know the climate is pessimistic. It's understandable after the crash. But the sky isn't falling and it's time to take courage and risk being optimistic. That's my investment strategy. Be a good steward, practice steady plodding, and the Lord brings the increase. You'll make sure to telephone me when the bairn is here, won't you? I'll say good night, Merry Christmas, and Happy New Year. Oh, and this is for you." He handed Michael an envelope.

"Merry Christmas to you, too, Ian," I said at last, entering the conversation from the sidelines. He took a smooth and silent stride to me, bowed to lift my hand and kiss it, then left the room, first taking a few steps backward, as if taking leave of royalty, and ever so gently closing the door. I was impressed with his deportment and his affection.

"I think Ian is Mr. Right," I said dreamily, my attention back on my kissed hand.

"What about me?" my dear husband wanted to know.

"You're *my* Mr. Right."

He gave me one of his winning smiles.

Chapter Twenty-five

Very Strong Tea

It is pleasant to labor for those we love.

Susana Cleveland's sampler

What a difference it makes to the soul to wake to sunshine in mid-January. A blue sky is so welcoming after the overshadowing of so many gray and gloomy days. I stood close to an easterly window in order to feel the gentle rays of morning sun through the glass, wishing it were enough to warm me completely and that I could do away with my thick wool cardigan—my constant companion that shielded me against the draughts of an old house. Wearing the same cardigan day in and day out was beginning to be irksome, but I didn't dare wear the one reserved for Sunday "best." Therefore I buttoned the top three buttons and started my day.

Michael and the children were already in the kitchen eating oatmeal with maple syrup. We exchanged good mornings. Emma had started bread rising. The woodstoves were fired up, but I still didn't feel warm. Michael saw me with my arms crossed over my chest above my tight bulging stomach and said, "The oatmeal is hot."

"Mmm, I like it with maple syrup," I said, but when I sat down to a bowl, all I could think about was wallpaper paste. I had no appetite. My lower back ached in my chair. I stirred the pastey oatmeal around and around, lackadaisically.

"You're going to stir the pattern off that plate in a minute," Michael said. Taking my cue, I put the spoon in my mouth.

"Mmm, creamy," I said, trying to show my appreciation that Emma made breakfast every morning. She and Michael were sipping their coffee with odd expressions.

Donald said, "We're going outside to take care of the chicken coop now, Dad, and to bring in more sticks." This announcement sounded like Michael had given the children a verbal checklist earlier that morning. I was very happy he had found a use for his managerial skills, and that he would be home all winter and doing some of the home teaching for a while.

"Good, son."

"Wear your old mittens for that chore, please," was my correction to Emily.

"Yes, Mom," she said. She slipped the red ones off and found her brown pair in the mitten basket.

Emma said, "It's good to see the sun after so many gray days, isn't it?"

"Yes, it's so welcoming," I replied, "The east side of a house is the perfect place for a kitchen to be."

"I've always thought so, too." Emma said.

Michael just listened. Being a man, he had most likely never given any thought to the matter. He emptied his coffee cup, and a minute later said, "If you aren't going to finish your oatmeal, I will."

I pushed the bowl across the table to him. The kitchen door opened and closed, the children's exit filling up the kitchen with cold air.

───❧❧───

It has always been "work before pleasure" at Blackberry Inn. The habit of paying heed to this Puritan motto kept me moving day by day without giving it a second thought. But today I recalled the motto with my eye on sitting before the woodstove with Emily. After we were released from chores, I planned to show her how to do what my mother had called "chicken scratch," that is, to put a cross stitch or a snowflake stitch in a pattern of squares of gingham fabric.

The anticipation of sitting before the woodstove with my daughter was the pleasure that kept me plodding through that morning, my carrot to draw me forward. I felt listless and chilled and thought of putting a shawl over my cardigan, but once I got up and moved about, I felt warmer. I drained the beans I had soaked overnight and added chopped onion, dark molasses, a jar of our summer tomatoes, a chunk of bacon, and a pinch of dry mustard and salt. Into the bean pot they went for eight hours of baking untouched. This was my tried and true recipe for beans that always turned out tender and flavorful. It was a favorite dish of Michael's and I had planned to make it especially for him. Next I filled the washer with water and did some clothes. The clothes were washed, put through the wringer, and placed on racks before the woodstove in one hour's time. In the batch of clothes were four flannel receiving blankets. "I wrapped you up in these," I told Emily.

"This one too, with the yellow chicks?" she asked.

"This one too, with the yellow chicks."

"Are you going to wrap your baby in it?"

"I'd like to," I said.

"She'll like it," Emily said.

Donald washed the kitchen floor. I knew the baby would be coming any day and wanted the house to be clean. Michael dust-mopped the floors as well as the baseboards, which were impossible for me to reach in my greatly expanded state. Emily and I dusted the furniture, with Emma helping. Otherwise dusting the big house would have taken longer than the wash. We started upstairs and worked our way toward the first floor where the radio was playing. This made our work lighter.

After a lunch of bread, farmer's cheese, and shredded baked cabbage, I collected everything from my bedroom that I needed in order to give Emily a lesson in cross stitch, and met her downstairs. Michael moved an easy chair close to the stove for me, but when I sat down, the ache in my back was stabbing. Then I woke to the thought that maybe my labor had begun, although I hadn't had back labor with my other children. I decided it was probably just my enormous size. I lay down on the sofa instead and, with the fabric in the hoop, showed Emily how cross stitch is done. She caught on quickly. "Yes, that's right," I said, "three squares, skip a square, and count three more for the top of the heart."

Her grandmother looked over her shoulder, and said, "Ooh, that yellow floss in the blue squares looks pretty!" When I stood up I must

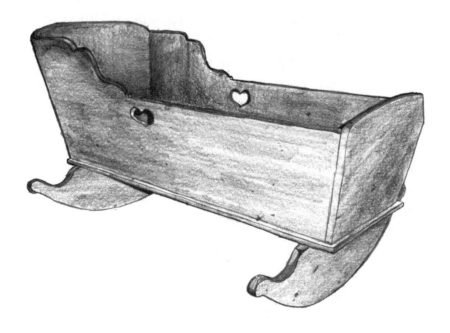

have had an alarmed look on my face, because Emma told Emily to go into her bedroom to fetch a hoop from her sewing table. "Carol, are you all right?" she asked, when Emily had trotted away.

"It's time. I'm going upstairs. Will you do the cross stitch with Emily?" I asked.

"Yes, dear."

Michael saw me climbing the stairs very slowly, leaning heavily onto the banister. He came to my side instantly so I could lean instead on his assisting arm. My thoughts went back to that bright and beautiful summer day when he had met me halfway down the stairs and taken my arm so that we could walk down together.

"Please make sure the children take their cod liver oil tonight," I said.

"I will," he said.

"And tell Emma that the baked beans should be done at five o'clock."

"Gotcha," he said.

~~~

Soon Emma appeared. She had a bed already set up for my special day in one of the sunny guest rooms. But the sun was gone and dark clouds had blown in, overshadowing the day so much that it seemed like bedtime to me. The snowflakes blew past the window, collecting in thick, furry clumps. A loud tweet brought me closer to the window. "Look, there's one of my cardinals!" I said, but when I turned around I found that I was alone in the room. The male cardinal was sitting on a branch. It shook the snow off itself, and flew away like a puff of red feathers in the wind. I wondered how many times it had visited that tree when I hadn't been watching. I got into bed and kept my eyes on the window for the female. Michael was downstairs on the telephone, notifying the doctor. A few minutes later I heard him and Emma talking on the landing, but my door was only half open, so I couldn't make out what they were saying.

The house became quiet. It was so quiet that it seemed as if it were empty of people. I could smell my beans baking. I was in a haze, dozing and dreaming without any consciousness of the passing of time, so that a minute might have been an hour and an hour a minute. A beautiful garden entered my dream, a garden of purple flowers—with a warm breeze gently stirring their scent. I lifted my head and looked around. On the nightstand sat a china bowl filled with a handful of dried lavender buds, mint leaves, rosemary, and scented geranium. The room was lit by firelight. I propped myself higher on the pillows with my elbows, only to be met with a tightening cramp, which awakened me to reality. I let my head fall back onto the pillow again. Closing my eyes, I willed myself back into the garden of purple flowers I had waiting for me. When the pain subsided, I opened my eyes to see a quiet figure enter the room. It was Emma carrying a folded blanket. Without speaking, she guided me to sit up even further, and I leaned forward so that she could tuck the blanket, which she had just warmed downstairs at the woodstove, into the small of my back. The warmth had a soothing power to enable me to sink into a moment of sweet relaxation until another wave of cramps gripped me.

"How long have I been dozing?" I asked her.

She would not tell me, but took the opportunity to share news of the doctor and the snowstorm. "Michael finally did reach the doctor, dearest, but he's in Warren taking over for another doctor there, and would never get here in time anyway. The snow is too deep. I'm watching over you. I assisted Dr. Cook many times with deliveries. I was with Penelope when she had Seth and when she had Sarah, too. She'd only been in Appleton five months when Seth was born. My, my, he was a stubborn one, just like this one."

I observed that it was nighttime. She saw me looking at the windows and said, "Michael and the children are in bed. If that baby doesn't come in another hour, I'll bring you up a cup of my labor tea. I found the herbs and have them next to the kettle. They work wonders to speed up a delivery that drags on. I make it with honey, so it will give you energy, too."

"Is it hot in here?" I asked.

"It's comfortably warm," she said.

She sat in a chair next to my bed and silently began working on her crochet with only the firelight to illuminate her white thread. She didn't tell me then, but I found out later that the electricity had gone off. Emma worked her crochet by feel more than by sight, anyway. Her fingers moved in rhythms, the thread gliding into place effortlessly. Now and again she would rise to poke the fire, or she would smooth the covers and the resting place of my head, wiping the perspiration off my brow, and then gently resume her seat beside me and pick up her crochet again. This activity was done in a rhythmic pattern, just as her fingers worked in their definite patterns to form their lace. The ritual went on for what seemed a long time before she disappeared and returned with an iron kettle of her strong brew of tea. She set the kettle on the fireplace crane to keep it warm, and tipped it over to pour me a cup.

"What did you put in here?" I asked, with my first timid sip. The tea was the temperature of bathwater, not very hot, and it was murky and bitter, in spite of all its honey. So much honey made it slimy. It was sickening.

"Angelica root, cohosh, and catnip. It's meant to be drunk in swallows rather than sips."

I drank it all but could barely keep it down. I waited and waited and then was brought two more cups of the disgusting brew. It was the third cup that turned my breathing into panting. "Your golden hour is here, dear. Let me help you out of bed. You need to stand up." She placed a strong arm behind me and held out her other hand.

It was utterly and entirely not my idea of the way to give birth, but out of respect for her experience, I did as I was told.

"Here, hold onto the end of the bed frame," she instructed, while guiding my hands to the spot. We stood together, side by side, me gripping the bed frame, squelching each desire to cry out, until the room brightened a little with the soft glow of early morning. Emma parted the drapes and pointed out the morning star. "A morning star over a snowy hill is always so pretty," she said.

"That tea is strong stuff," I said, living in a different world than she did at that moment.

"So are you, Carol," she encouraged, "just a bit longer and you can get back into bed."

"It's always work before pleasure," I murmured, and turned my attention back to my task with all of my might.

～～

I heard my children's voices on the landing and their galloping footsteps, and then a strong, drawn out "hush" from Michael. They were going downstairs for breakfast.

～～

Emma placed his tiny body in my arms. "Isn't he beautiful? What will you call him?"

"Michael and I agreed upon Eliot, after John Eliot, the missionary."

"That's a fine name."

"Thank you, Emma, I mean, thank you for all your help." My private thought was, "You're a peach."

"You're very welcome. I love babies." She was tidying the washstand, making the room look presentable. She brought in fresh linen, a clean blanket, and even laid a different quilt across the foot of the bed. I could keep my secret no longer. While I kept my gaze upon Eliot's tiny delicate face I recited a line of her poem, "It takes a heap o' living in a house t' make it home."

She stopped what she was doing, turned, and looked at me with compassionate eyes. "Yes, yes it does," she agreed. Then, from memory she spoke the lines that followed:

> *Within the wall there's got to be some babies born, and*
> > *then*
> *Right there you've got to bring them up to women good,*
> > *and men;*
> *And gradually, as time goes on, you find you wouldn't part*
> *With anything they ever used—they're grown into your*
> > *heart:*

The old high chairs, the playthings, too, the little shoes
they wore
You hoard; and if you could you'd keep the thumb-marks
on the door.

Halfway through this recitation she continued her tidying. Failing at her attempt to sufficiently stifle a large yawn, she walked out the door with an oversized bundle of wash under her arm. I knew she was going to bring the news to Michael and the children. It was then that my emotions surfaced as Eliot's eyes found mine for the first time. They were dark dreamy eyes and his headful of hair was dark, too, inherited from his father. The meeting was blissful. "Hello sweetie pie," I spoke. "Thank you for this beautiful baby," was my prayer to my heavenly Father. A moment later I heard the clamor of running feet up the stairs and Michael's commanding call, "Whoa, hold your horses. Wait for me." He wanted to be first to enter. He turned the knob slowly and poked his head in the door to ask in his gentlemanly way, "May we come in?"

"Please, " I said. Michael entered, and bent over the bed to kiss me, then the cheek of our baby. "Hello, Eliot," he said. He wiggled a finger into the baby's tiny hand and the baby held onto it. "I'm so happy," he told me.

"I am, too," I said. "He looks like you."

"I wouldn't mind one bit if they all looked like you," Michael said. Then he turned to the children and said, "Come and meet your brand new brother."

Donald fixed his eyes on the baby's face, and said with the vigor of an optimist, "I knew it would be a boy." This made Emily want to get even. She said, "Next time it will be a girl, right, Mommy?" She was holding the yellow receiving blanket in her hand.

The End

Author's Chatterbox

Autumn 2008

The Village Blacksmith
by Henry Wadsworth Longfellow (1807–1882)

Under a spreading chestnut tree
    The village smithy stands;
The smith, a mighty man is he,
    With large and sinewy hands;
And the muscles of his brawny arms
    Are strong as iron bands.

His hair is crisp, and black, and long
    His face is like the tan;
His brow is wet with honest sweat,
    He earns whate'er he can,
And looks the whole world in the face,
    For he owes not any man.

Week in, week out, from morn till night,
    You can hear his bellows blow;
You can hear him swing his heavy sledge,
    With measured beat and slow,
Like a sexton ringing the village bell,
    When the evening sun is low.

And children coming home from school
 Look in at the open door;
They love to see the flaming forge,
 And hear the bellows roar,
And catch the burning sparks that fly
 Like chaff from a threshing-floor.

He goes on Sunday to the church,
 And sits among his boys;
He hears the parson pray and preach,
 He hears his daughter's voice,
Singing in the village choir,
 And it makes his heart rejoice.

It sounds to him like her mother's voice,
 Singing in Paradise!
He needs must think of her once more,
 How in the grave she lies;
And with his hard, rough hand he wipes
 A tear out of his eyes.

Toiling,—rejoicing,—sorrowing,
 Onward through life he goes;
Each morning sees some task begin,
 Each evening sees it close;
Something attempted, something done,
 Has earned a night's repose.

Thanks, thanks to thee, my worthy friend,
 For the lesson thou hast taught!
Thus at the flaming forge of life
 Our fortunes must be wrought;
Thus on its sounding anvil shaped
 Each burning deed and thought.

Apple Butter Making

The painting "Apple Butter Making" by Grandma Moses gave me the idea to have an Apple Butter Festival in Appleton. It depicts one of a variety of activities from Grandma Moses' childhood when work was accompanied by play. In her autobiography, *My Life's History*, Grandma Moses wrote, "The apple butter was considered a necessity." The festival appealed to Michael's enterprising schemes to attract more tourists to the country as it gave him a reason for advertising. During the Depression years, if there was one thing the country had that  the city lacked, it was food—produced by hard work and the work was constant. Chores were governed by gender, age, and the calendar. The schedule of chores was orderly, both for the days of the week and the seasons of the year.

Mr. Fortesque makes the comment that he wants his niece Siobhan to witness women who willingly work with their hands, women who wear strength and honor as their clothing. This Christian ethic was derived from the lifestyle of the woman of Proverbs who looked to the ways of her household. The modern mother, who has decided to home teach, can relate to this hard work. Her work is constant. It also is scheduled by the hour and the seasons of the year. Chores can be shared, however, and many hands make light work. My son, Nigel, has been my floor boy. Like Donald he washes the kitchen floor for me—and a very good use of muscle it is. Remembering to schedule in a time of recreation and play benefits all who work. Penelope told Dora that having something so pleasant as Dora's tea to look forward to, helped make her days of canning go more easily.

Apple Butter Making in the Crock-Pot

Here is my shortcut recipe for apple butter. I made it the day before my extended family came to visit. When any of the family wandered into the kitchen while I was preparing a meal for them, as they often do unconsciously when hungry, I put a spoonful of my apple butter in their mouth, and said, "What do you think?"

"This is fantastic," they would say, eyebrows raised. It was funny to see each face when the spoonful of flavor reached the senses.

"What is it?" they would ask.

"It's my apple butter."

Easy Old-Fashioned Apple Butter

4 cups of unsweetened applesauce
1 cup of apple cider
2/3 cup of root beer (or less)
A pinch of ground cloves, nutmeg, and allspice
Two pinches of cinnamon

————

The root beer sweetens the recipe sufficiently so that no sugar is needed.

This recipe makes one-and-a-half cups of rich dark apple butter.

————

You could boil the cider rapidly for thirty minutes on the stove, to reduce it, before adding it to the Crock-Pot. This shortens cooking time in the Crock-Pot, but I added all the ingredients without this step because I wanted to make a good start on the other cooking I had to do that day. Therefore I let the ingredients simmer most of the day on low heat, stirring with a wooden spoon now and again. The way to tell when the apple butter is ready is to put some on the center of a saucer and tilt. If the butter is runny, it needs more cooking time. When done, it should be thick and take on a rich dark color.

Twenty to thirty minutes before I remove the apple butter from the Crock-Pot, I add my spices. I use a little of all the pumpkin pie spices but ginger.

————

The root beer I used was Virgil's micro-brewed. The bottle said it was flavored with a hint of anise and wintergreen. The menfolk of my family are especially fond of root beer, so this recipe appealed to their tastes. An Amish family brews their own root beer in Bird-in-Hand, a few towns away from where we live. Just this month Dean stopped along the roadside to purchase a cold bottle to share with me. It was delicious. Next time I make apple butter, I will make it with their brew and be sure to double my recipe if I am expecting my extended family for the weekend.

———

Keep your jar of apple butter in the refrigerator.

Autumn Apple Butter from Apples

This recipe can also be made in your Crock-Pot and is a good one for using farm stand apples that are "seconds," or for using whatever apples are available at the grocer's. Red or Golden Delicious and bottled cider make a mixture that is very pleasing. This recipe makes five cups of apple butter.

———

1-1/2 quarts cider
8 apples, cored, peeled (optional), and cut into quarters
1 cup or less of brown sugar (sweeten to taste)
1 teaspoon each of ground cloves and cinnamon
½ teaspoon allspice
½ teaspoon salt

———

Boil the cider rapidly, uncovered, for thirty minutes to reduce by half. Pile apples into the Crock-Pot. They should nearly fill the pot. Add the hot cider and set the heat on low. Cook about eight hours, using a wooden spoon to stir and break up the apples every half hour or so.

After about four hours, add the sugar by parts, tasting for sweetness. During the last half hour, add spices and salt. When apples have cooked to a thick mash, smooth the mixture in a blender or food processor. Keep jars in the refrigerator.

Carol's Apple Butter Muffins

I found an old recipe for apple butter cake and adjusted it for muffins. Perhaps these ought to be called cupcakes, because they are  a little lighter and sweeter than muffins. They taste so scrumptious that I decided to write them into my story and make them a childhood favorite of Carol's. Muffins and cupcakes freeze well so you might wish to double the recipe.

Preheat oven to 350 degrees.

Grease muffin tins with butter for one dozen muffins.

––––––––

1 cup of light brown sugar
½ cup of butter at room temperature
2 eggs
1 cup of apple butter
¾ cup buttermilk
2 cups of unbleached flour
2 teaspoons of aluminum-free baking soda
1 teaspoon each ground cinnamon, cloves, nutmeg, allspice

––––––––

In a large mixing bowl cream together sugar and butter. Beat in eggs. Mix in apple butter and buttermilk.

Sift flour mixture into a separate bowl, then add this to the creamed mixture stirring lightly just until moistened.

Fill muffin tins.

Place in center of oven and bake for 20 to 25 minutes.

Carol's Salmon Croquettes

English settlers brought the practice of serving minced seafood patties to the colonies. The croquette is an economical way to feed a family and stretch ingredients. The amount of ingredients are intuitive: enough eggs and bread for binding the other ingredients, enough potato to stretch the fish you have on hand, enough fresh garden herbs to flavor.

I've made croquettes to use up the fish entrée I cooked the day before, leftover halibut or leftover fresh salmon. I have also made croquettes with canned salmon. They can also be made with leftover minced chicken. Cooking an entire bunch of parsley and bunch of green onion, until soft, in olive oil and butter, creates the necessary garden flavoring for this dish.

For a colorful country spread, serve croquettes with sliced ripe red tomatoes, corn chowder, butternut squash, and green salad.

This recipe makes about 14 croquettes to serve 5-6 people. If hungry growing boys sit at your table, this may require doubling the recipe.

---

2 6-oz cans wild Alaskan pink salmon or leftover fish, free of all bones
3 eggs
3 small to medium potatoes (2 white, 1 yam)
2 to 3 slices of light wheat bread, crumbled or torn into small pieces
1 bunch parsley, rinsed and chopped
1 bunch green onions, rinsed and cut in small pieces
Butter and olive oil (green olive oil is most flavorful)
2 heaping tablespoons of plain yogurt
A squeeze of lemon juice
A pinch or two of paprika or seafood seasoning (optional)
Salt

Cook onions on medium heat in a pan with a pat of butter and a short pour of olive oil. Add parsley partway through cooking. Cook gently until soft.

Feel free to use leftover mashed potatoes, but if not available simply microwave 2 small white, 1 yam. When the cooked potatoes are cool enough to handle, peel away the skins. The orange yam accentuates the pink color of salmon, but is optional. Mash potatoes and mix with egg, yogurt, a squeeze of lemon, and a pinch of paprika.

Mix in drained salmon, parsley and onion.

Add enough breadcrumbs for a firm consistency. Form into balls, then press into patties.

———

Preheat a large heavy skillet. Add oil to a preheated pan to coat. Carefully place patties in pan. Cook on medium heat. Lightly brown on each side, turning carefully. I always find it necessary to add a tad more olive oil to my skillet during cooking.

———

Arrange on dish and sprinkle with salt.

———

A rich sauce such as Mornay Sauce, made with Gruyère cheese, butter, and half and half will make a croquette elegant enough for a dinner party or fit for a king. Should I admit that I serve my family fish croquettes with ketchup or tartar sauce? My husband, Dean, likes me to set a jar of chutney on the table.

Emma's Vegetable Cheese Pie

Emma mentioned that it was an Italian guest of Blackberry Inn who gave her basil seeds. The fragrance of fresh basil brings back memories to my father of his childhood summers. Dad grew up in an Italian neighborhood in New Jersey, fifteen miles from Manhattan, surrounded by extended family. The houses were close together and arranged in blocks. There was a place, however, on the block where no houses stood and the immigrants had permission to grow their lush vegetable gardens. While his own mother worked in a dress factory, it was his grandmother who got him to do hours of garden chores in the hot sun, hauling water from the well uphill in a bucket, weeding, etc. Grandma fed the neighborhood. What she grew, she cooked, leaving meals seasoned with basil regularly at the doorsteps of the ill and elderly. Each morning she attended Mass and was the matriarch of those who ate macaroni in her basement. A summer kitchen lined one side of the basement. It made a cooler environment to can tomatoes, to boil macaroni, and to eat. It provided plenty of room for those who came down the cement steps to gossip or bicker loudly in Italian about news.

Basil is a beautifully leafed annual herb, easily started by seed in warmer climates. The leaves are shiny and smooth. Basil is a member of the mint family and quite fragrant. Pinch off the top leaves of the plant to use in a summer dish. Let one plant go to flower and then to seed. These seeds can be saved for the following spring's sowing. Basil dries readily. Italians, on my husband's side of the family, filled jars full of dried basil to flavor pizza  and pasta dishes. Freshly grated hard cheese is a world apart in flavor from the pre-grated cheese in the carton. Give a hunk of hard cheese three passes over the grater and it tops a dish with plenty of snowy savory cheese that melts in your mouth and mingles with the other flavors of the dish rather than overpowering them.

"Pot cheese" is a kind of Italian cottage cheese made on the kitchen counter. You know it as ricotta. Cottage cheese, however, can be used with this dish if it is first put in a blender to smooth the curds.

———

To Make One 9-inch Pie:

16 ounces of ricotta cheese

A large sprig of basil leaves—several handfuls washed, chopped, left raw

1 egg

½ cup of freshly grated parmesan, Romano or asiago cheese

One bag of fresh baby spinach, rinsed well

> Place the wet spinach leaves in a saucepan and heat only until the leaves wilt. When cool, squeeze out excess water and chop. (A package of frozen chopped spinach, thawed and squeezed, works too. My primitive method is to let the water run through my fingers as I squeeze the frozen spinach one handful at a time.)

1 tomato
Salt and pepper to taste
Butter to grease a pie pan
(Optional) several sprigs of chopped green onion cooked until
    soft in olive oil and butter.
(Optional) pie crust

———

Preheat oven to 350 degrees.

In a large mixing bowl, crack egg, add salt and pepper. Mix thoroughly with ricotta. Fold in basil, grated hard cheese, green onion, and lastly, the chopped spinach. Spoon mixture into a greased pie pan. Decorate on top with thin slices of tomato. A pie crust doubles my time in the kitchen so I do without it. I'd rather get my fatty calories from some crusty bread dipped in olive oil, salt, and garlic.

Bake in the oven for 20 to 35 minutes.

Serve with salad, crusty bread, minestrone soup, or lentil soup.

———

Emma added sliced summer squash to her pie.

For special occasions I have doubled the same ricotta/spinach recipe (eliminating the green onion) for filling jumbo macaroni shells.

Carol's Cornbread at the Hearth

Carol's cornbread can be made anytime there are leaves on the trees. The moist maple leaves serve as parchment paper and create

a design on the cornbread. The stems of the leaves make good handles for children to use in removing the leaves from the hot corn bread. Because leaves are used, the crust of the bread is not crispy the way it would be when batter is poured into a well-greased, preheated (sizzling hot) iron skillet and baked. This is the way my southern friends like it most often, and I do, too. But by using leaves, I found that the pan washes up in a breeze.

Do you have a brick fireplace and an iron Dutch oven? If so, you could cook your cornbread the way Carol did. A Dutch oven usually has legs, allowing you to rake the hot embers underneath and around the oven. A fireplace needs preheating. The wood needs to be burning for more than an hour before it creates embers for cooking.

As a side note, I've placed Idaho potatoes onto hot embers. Cooked in the fireplace, the potatoes are scrumptious. Pierce skins first with a fork and wrap each potato in parchment paper (or leaves) before covering with aluminum foil. Remove from fire with long prongs and oven mitts. Potatoes can also be placed into a Dutch oven.

————

Line the bottom of a 9x9 inch baking dish or cake pan with maple leaves placed front side down. Preheat conventional oven to 400 degrees.

————

Sift together in a large mixing bowl:
1 cup unbleached flour
4 teaspoons aluminum-free baking powder
¾ teaspoon salt
Wisk in: 1 cup yellow cornmeal
¼ cup sugar
(Optional—a pinch of nutmeg)

————

In a separate bowl mix:
1 cup whole milk (warmed slightly in microwave)
¼ cup melted butter (drizzle into warm milk to mix)
2 eggs

————

Combine wet ingredients with dry, using a few strong strokes, mixing just until moistened.

Pour batter onto maple leaves, using a spatula to scrap every last drop from the bowl.

Bake in conventional oven for 20 to 25 minutes or until center springs to the touch.

Let the cornbread cool slightly and then, with potholders, turn the pan over onto a wooden cutting board. Young children will enjoy peeling off the leaves by their stems to see the design. Cut into wedges and serve outdoors or assign the chore of sweeping crumbs to a floor boy.

Carol's Winter Baked Beans

Carol cooked beans the day before she delivered Eliot. Beans used to be a staple in the American diet. The wide cooking fireplaces of Colonial America sometimes had beehive ovens hidden within them. Today colonial revivalists are building these same dome-shaped mortar ovens into the sides of their large fireplaces. Baked beans were traditionally made in a clay pot. A fire was built in the beehive oven, and when the wood was reduced to embers and the bricks were good and warmed, the bean pot was set inside to gently simmer all night. The oldest recipe I have does not call for tomato. Carol knew Michael liked his beans with tomato, and since tomato has become the traditional flavor of this dish, I include it here. You may use pea, lima, or navy beans. The Indians introduced the settlers to white beans. These were taken aboard ship for sailors to eat and became our navy bean. Navy beans take the longest to soften. Lima beans are less tough. Pea beans are smaller and are typically the bean used in New England. You can use any dried bean of your choice.

––––––––

One pound or two cups dried beans. Rinse and pick over beans. Soak beans overnight in water to cover by two inches. Drain beans in the morning. At breakfast place the presoaked beans in a pot on the stove, cover with water to parboil. Simmer for thirty minutes. Meanwhile add to your Crock-Pot the following ingredients and set the heat on low.

––––––––

1 to 2 onions, chopped
2 tablespoons dark molasses
2 – 4 tablespoons brown sugar
1 quart tomato juice

1 teaspoon each salt and dry mustard

A pinch of ground cloves and/or a pinch of cumin

(Optional) half a pound of salt pork, scored, or a half a pound
of sausage meat, or bacon cut in chunks.

————

While the beans are simmering on the stove and the sauce is in
the pot, sit down to enjoy your breakfast. Thirty minutes later, when
you are finished with breakfast, drain parboiled beans and add them
to your Crock-Pot of sauce. Let the beans simmer anywhere from four
to six hours or until beans are soft and sauce is starchy. Check the
beans only occasionally to make sure they are covered with sauce,
adding more tomato juice if necessary. More molasses or brown sugar
may be added to your taste near the end of cooking.

Beeswax and Honey

I have two long-distance friends, Sue and Cheryl, who live at opposite ends of America, and who keep bees in their back yard. They eat
the honey, but leave the wax so that the bees can hang onto their building material. Honey is one of nature's purest foods. Sue told me that a
bee produces only half a teaspoon of honey in its lifetime. Therefore,
a spoonful of honey is two lifetimes. And a spoonful is what I reached
for on the day I wrote about Carol's outing to the Candlewycks.

Perhaps a family near you keeps bees and would invite you into
their back yard to tell you and your children about them. I've read
that honeybees were rare in Colonial America and that most candles
were made with tallow, the fat of sheep or cattle, and didn't smell so
very nice. The process of melting the wax off of bayberries involved
the tedious skimming off of what floated to the top of the kettle.
These bayberry candles had a fragrance that was pleasant, but for
most housewives they were not worth the work. My favorite candle is
made of beeswax. It makes the house smell of honey. Nigel's drawing
of the candle mold was taken from my antique mold. I've never used
it. Instead I have dipped candles and given them as gifts.

Children's Books

Speaking of honey, my children enjoyed reading *Winnie the Pooh*, by A. A. Milne. It was one of the first chapter books that my daughter, Sophia, read silently. She had had little knowledge of the Disney cartoons at the time of her reading, and so her images of the characters were not influenced as much by the cartoons, as her own imagination, as is typical when we read a book. And yes, I did let her read it as a schoolbook. *Winnie the Pooh* is one of those books that has stood the test of time and has thus become a children's classic. It has been loved by persons of all ages for generations. A friend of mine

shared with me something that she found funny. She caught her eldest son—a bearded young man standing over six feet tall, and engaged to be married—chuckling on the window seat, the family's copy of *Winnie the Pooh* open before him. As a young child he had read about the antics of Pooh and the peculiarities of his friends. He had thought he would only take a passing glance at the story he had loved so well, but had ended up reading the whole book, and admitted to enjoying it with a mature appreciation. Charlotte Mason said that having read a really good book once, we have only breakfasted.

The other children's classics mentioned in this story have also been ones our family has enjoyed.

Nigel's Illustrations

My son, Nigel, wanted to draw characters into his illustrations. I told him that my readers would create their own characters' faces. "Book illustrations are boring without people," he moaned. The domestic subjects I gave him furthered his disinterest. His own subjects of choice are action heroes, shady characters, and aliens living on strange planets. In fact, an intricate alien landscape done in watercolor won him first prize at the country fair just prior to taking on my challenge.

"I can assure you that my readers will not find your pictures as boring as you think. Mothers will find these domestic scenes soothing and attractive," I told him. He remained unconvinced, but kept drawing the subjects I required of him, such as a tea service and a table of pie shells ready to be filled. "I'll throw in a car. How's that? Just be sure to make the background Appleton and not Mars." This appeased him for the time being, until I threw another domestic subject at him. If you look closely, you will see that Nigel couldn't resist sneaking some people into the background of a few of his pictures. I approved, since they were tiny.

One dark winter evening I carried my laptop computer into Nigel's bedroom and began reading aloud to him one of my chapters. Halfway into the first paragraph he cut me off. "Stop, stop, it's too corny."

"But I'm having trouble assigning you an illustration for this chapter, and I was hoping you'd help me come up with an idea."

He was at a complete loss. It was no use. "No, Mom. I'm sorry. Your book is far too domestic. Please don't read anymore. I can't bear it."

"You've been reading far too much Edgar Rice Burroughs," I said, pretending to be cross and insulted. That winter his father had picked up a stack of paperback Tarzan novels at a used bookshop. These novels are saturated with fast action, heroism, and exotic adventure— the sort of thing young men relish.

"I can't put them down," he confessed, a little apologetically. So because my story could hold no interest for him, Nigel illustrated my chapters without reading them.

———

Nigel's illustration of Emma's secretary is my secretary, feather pen and all. The feather is from one of the many wild turkeys that sauntered across our lawn when we lived in Maine. I spotted some turkeys here in Lancaster Country, Pennsylvania, this year and was surprised. Behind the secretary's rounded glass are some of my favorite books, pincushions, and sundry keepsakes. I stacked some of my books in a pyramid beside my bed for Nigel to draw. It took only minutes to collect them because we have so many. I am guessing that you also have lots of books in your house and rely upon them for guidance, encouragement, and relaxation, as I have done all during my years of home teaching. The large book in the illustration, placed at the bottom of the pile—*Famous Paintings*—is the same one Carol used. Although I like the commentary by G.K. Chesterton, I don't suggest searching high and low for it, because a myriad of other art print books await you and are more conveniently available. Such books feature the artwork of one artist or of a particular school of art. Carol foregoes a mention that *Famous Paintings* includes more than several nudes.

One of my favorite illustrations of Nigel's is the toy tea party with Raggedy Ann. When my daughter Sophia saw the picture, she recognized the back of her large Teddy. Nigel used the head of this antique-style Teddy she had made for me years prior. It has buttoned hinged arms and legs, and gets rather dusty sitting on my furniture. Every few months I take him outside and give him a regular beating to free him of dust, making sure that none of the Amish children who play next door witness this violent act.

Nigel used an Ashford spinning wheel—the Elizabeth—as his model for Dora's wheel. My wheel is the Ashford Traditional.

The silhouette couple at the foot of Emma's attic stairs is similar to one I have on my wall. I never worked into my story who this couple is but in my imagination they are Emma's grandparents when first married.

I don't have a tea set as beautiful as the one Nigel drew. I gave him a page from a magazine to use as a guide. The colors of the design on the cups and saucers are raspberry, burgundy, and cream.

What do you think of the rope swing? Does it look inviting? We once rented a house in Oregon long ago that came with a rope swing attached way up on the high branch of an oak tree. The autumn we moved into the house, our children were just at the right age to enjoy sailing through the air on it. Since then we have never found one to match it.

Blackberries on the Cover

When designing the simple cross-stitched cover of the book, I decided to stitch a blackberry flower in each corner. I wanted to make sure what they looked like, so I walked out our back door into our back yard, where a good many bushes happened to be in full bloom. It was May, and blackberries are a May flower in Pennsylvania. Later I had to pick out the white flowers and make them into blackberries. That little patch of white in each corner did not show up when scanned into the computer.

I worked another sampler so you could see what Carol's fictional girlhood sampler looked like. "Be ye always kind and true" was worked by Carol Young with her needle at age eleven. I hope to place a photograph of it on our website, Homeschool Highlights. Phrases like this one were derived from the New England Primer and Scripture and were featured on samplers during the eighteenth and nineteenth centuries.

One of my favorite rhyming phrases is "Let wisdom every step attend, and virtue be my constant friend." My long-distance friend, Susana, has stitched a collection of beautiful early American samplers on linen—just one of the ways she beautifies her home while displaying mottos for righteous living. Susana is a domestic artist-extraordinaire. Hearing about her samplers inspired me to make my own. I still knit, and I enjoy knitting little sweaters for my grandson, and other grandchildren I may have in the future. I knit and keep my finished projects stored in my Grandmother's Someday Box. I like to make fabric yo-yos, too.

My Cardinals

One October morning I spotted a male and female cardinal outside my bedroom window. They were pecking the dry blackberries that were clinging to the low branches. It was their tweets that alerted me that they were close by. This cardinal-couple looked haggard and worn and were followed into the bushes by two fledglings.

I was in bed for an entire summer and autumn before I began writing down this story, a story I had been keeping in the back of my mind for over a year, during which time our two daughters were married and many busy days passed. Just after the second wedding, I fell apart with a number of ailments. This led me to see a number of doctors. I had blood tests, a biopsy, was put on various medications, and was given physical therapy. Here it was, my first September of no home teaching and I was in bed.

To pass the time I knitted, read, and listened to Christian radio. Every day my cardinals kept me company. The trees beside this little house we are renting are less than ten feet from my bedroom window. When I spotted one cardinal on a branch, I usually saw its mate, too. They tweeted at dawn and later in the afternoon, either perching or darting to and fro, providing me with glimpses of an outdoor theatre. I managed to attract them to stay in the same woods all autumn and winter with sunflower seeds in a squirrel-proof bird feeder. Dean purchased it for me, hung it up on the back deck, and kept it filled.

On some days my cardinals were the only incentive I had for getting out of bed. Soon the entire deck became a bird feeder, attracting more birds that I looked forward to seeing day by day. What a mess they made! The feeder was in view of the kitchen. Eating was also a trial for me, but sharing a meal with my trustworthy cardinals eventually helped me regain my strength and courage. Remarkably, the birds had similar mealtimes to ours. By the way, to eat like a bird is to eat several times one's body weight in a day. A horse, in contrast, doesn't come close to eating its body weight in a day. It made me wonder how each simile got started.

Another autumn has arrived and in fact is already drawing to a close. As my writing of *Blackberry Inn* also comes to a close, the cardinals tweet most mornings at sunrise, and are one of few birds left singing in our woods. By the time this book is out the door of the printer's, we should be out of this rented house and moved into our own house down the road. I'll be leaving my cardinal family behind. Perhaps I'll connect with another family of feathered companions.

A Real Man and Health

In my story, Ian Fortesque spends time at one of Bernarr Macfadden's health resorts. In the late 1940s and early 1950s, Dean's grandfather, Salvatore DeSalvo—along with his wife, Josephine—stayed at Bernarr Macfadden's majestic health resort in Dansville, New York. Here's a bit of trivia: The first cold cereal was invented in Dansville by Dr. James Caleb Jackson. You know this healthy cereal as granola. Anyway, Dean's grandparents kept a large vegetable garden and tried to live by Mr. Macfadden's writings. We have black and white 8mm movie film of Grandpa Sal joking around with Mr. Macfadden. Mr. Macfadden is holding Dean's sister on his shoulders, while they all wave at the camera. Grandpa Sal lived a healthy life to the age of 94.

Attending Mr. Macfadden's health resort would have taught Ian Fortesque that healthy living involves eating more fruits and vegetables than most Americans are accustomed to eating. It also involves regular exercise and fresh air, two things that Ian decided to take to heart. He even gave up coffee and, eventually, tobacco. These were part of his efforts to become the man he thought he should be for Emma, the woman he loved.

The newspapers and magazines owned by Mr. Macfadden had the world's largest circulation. He became a strong voice in American politics and used his *Liberty Magazine* to combat communism and promote free enterprise and low taxes for a strong working nation. In my story Ian was also a capitalist, and like Mr. Macfadden, helped start soup kitchens for the needy.

We have a small suitcase of old issues of *Liberty Magazine*. I researched an issue from the year my story takes place (1937-38) and found Mr. Macfadden's article debunking President Roosevelt's New Deal. Months after I wrote the dinner discussion into my story, the stock market took a serious dive and the government again started to "fix" things. To use a cliché, history repeats itself.

Edible Wild Plants

I pulled a book off the shelf of our local library that struck my fancy. It was the *Peterson Field Guide—Edible Wild Plants.* In it Mr. Lee Allen Peterson mentions a large mushroom that I remember seeing in my youth. Behind my childhood home in New Jersey is Washington Rock State Park. From here George Washington watched the movements of the British. I learned later that reconnaissance was achieved by observing the dust clouds that formed from the trail of men and horses. The children of our little neighborhood at the top of this rocky mountainside played in the shady woods.

I remember spotting a massive mushroom growing along the bark of a deciduous tree that Mr. Peterson's field guide says is *Polyporus sulpureus.* He says that the bright yellow and orange colors make it impossible to misidentify. On the same page he mentions the giant puffball and the morel mushroom. Leafing through the book, I also decided to include in my story the wild parsnip and *Helianthus tuberso-sus,* the Jerusalem Artichoke. (The common sunflower is closely named: *Helianthus annuus.*) It is the artichoke that is dug up by Darby in our story. I find it curious that my 1975 copy of *Joy of Cooking* includes a recipe for the Jerusalem Artichoke. It suggests simmering these tubers only until fork-tender, about fifteen minutes.

A Requirement for Home Teaching

Show me a mother with an enduring love for her children and I'll show you a mother who meets the requirements for home teaching. With love comes the self-sacrifice, daily discipline, kindness, patience, and determination needed to set her children's feet on the paths of righteousness, skill, and knowledge. She who sows seeds by home teaching, overtime will reap the fruits of her labor. My three children who are now grown—all studied at home to grade twelve. I am no longer their teacher and yet I relive those days on the pages of this book. This is probably because although they were exhausting years, they were some of the *best* years of my life. If the words of Miss Charlotte Mason sound intriguing and you would like to ponder more of her ideas, I recommend my book, *A Charlotte Mason Companion–Personal Reflection on the Gentle Art of Learning.*

A Sequel

I should mention that *Lessons at Blackberry Inn* is a sequel to *Pocketful of Pinecones.* Although *Pocketful of Pinecones* is the first in the series, it is not necessary to read it first. I tried to make this story stand on its own. I enjoy these chats with you, my readers, at the end of my fiction books. It is not typically done, but as my publisher is my husband, he lets this author do as she likes.

Topics for Personal Reflection or Group Discussion

I have listed some topics for building up sisters in the Lord. All of these topics can be traced back to characters or scenes in my story. Some of the topics are especially dear to me. At different times in my life I have pondered them. My opinion on them continues to develop as I mature. Rather than pose questions, I will allow you to consider what meaning each topic has in your life.

Perhaps an older woman in the Lord will use *Lessons at Blackberry Inn* to provide topics for discussion in a lady's parlor. Older women in the church are to be encouragers to the younger women, offering

friendly discipleship. Over tea, sympathy and practical advice can be shared about a myriad of things: how to love a husband; how to educate a child; how to cook something new and healthy; how to do needlework, how to create the home atmosphere we all crave; or maybe how to provide radiant hospitality as Emma does.

If you feel so nudged to lead a discussion on any of these topics, you will be able to make the discussion personal by simply posing the questions that come to mind. You know the ladies you desire to minister to, what their needs are, and where their interests lie, better than I.

How to love a husband
How to love children
Reading aloud
Narration—the art of knowing
Observing nature—getting outdoors
Beautiful pictures
Beautiful music
Kitchen ministry—mealtimes
Hospitality—celebrations
Chores—doing the "next thing"
Friendship and its place in the Christian religion
Trusting in Providence
Strength and honor as a woman's clothing
Needle arts
Giving handmade gifts
The poem "Home," by Edgar Guest
Charlotte Mason's advice in *Home Education*
The sorrow of a miscarriage or all "missed" children
The joy of a newborn baby

Publisher's Resources

Charlotte Mason Research & Supply
P.O. Box 296
Quarryville, Pennsylvania 17566
www.homeschoolhighlights.com

Karen Andreola's

Pocketful of Pinecones

Nature Study with the Gentle Art of Learning

A Story for Mother Culture™

Pocketful of Pinecones
Nature Study with the Gentle Art of Learning™
A Story for Mother Culture™
by Karen Andreola, 272 pages
ISBN: 1-889209-03-1

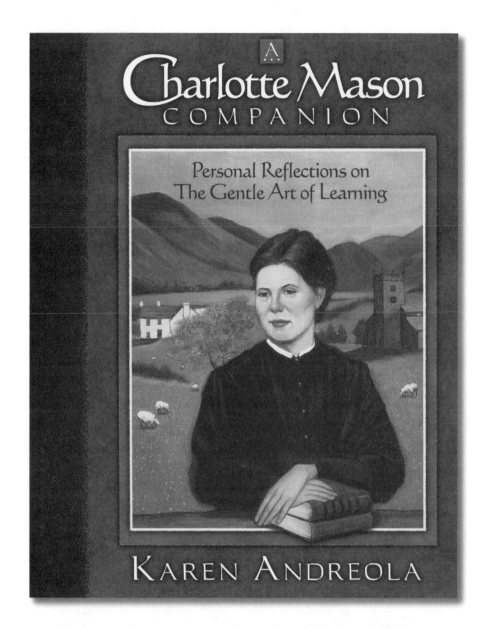

A Charlotte Mason Companion
Personal Reflections on the Gentle Art of Learning™
by Karen Andreola, 374 pages
beautifully illustrated
ISBN: 1-889209-02-3

Simply Grammar
An Illustrated Primer
by Karen Andreola, 178 pages
Victorian illustrations
ISBN: 1-889209-01-5

The Original Homeschooling Series
by Charlotte Mason, 2400 pages, 6-vol. set
ISBN: 1-889209-00-7

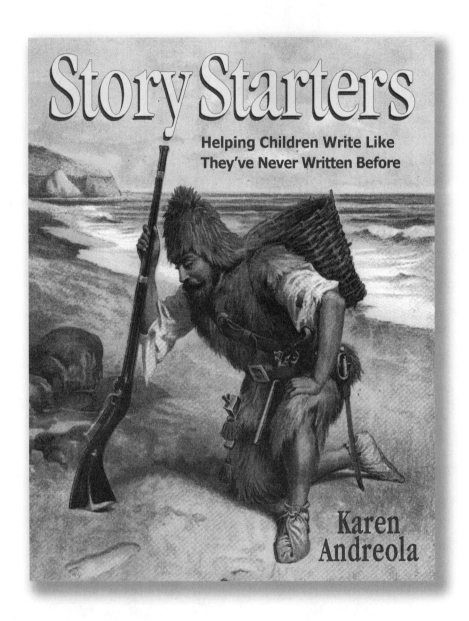

Story Starters
Helping Children Write Like
They've Never Written Before
by Karen Andreola, 460 pages
One book per family • Non-consumable • Lavishly illustrated
Multi-skill level (grade 4-12) • Supplementary English course
ISBN: 1-889209-04-X